AF662021

RAMAYANA AT A GLANCE

RAMAYANA
AT A GLANCE

SADGURU SANT KESHAVADAS

MOTILAL BANARSIDASS PUBLISHERS
PRIVATE LIMITED • DELHI (INDIA)

2nd Reprint: Delhi, 2015
First Published in USA in 1976
First Indian Edition: Delhi, 1988

© MOTILAL BANARSIDASS PUBLISHERS PRIVATE LIMITED
All Rights Reserved.

ISBN: 978-81-208-0545-3

MOTILAL BANARSIDASS
41 U.A. Bungalow Road, Jawahar Nagar, Delhi 110 007
8 Mahalaxmi Chamber, 22 Bhulabhai Desai Road, Mumbai 400 026
203 Royapettah High Road, Mylapore, Chennai 600 004
236, 9th Main III Block, Jayanagar, Bengaluru 560 011
Sanas Plaza, 1302 Baji Rao Road, Pune 411 002
8 Camac Street, Kolkata 700 017
Ashok Rajpath, Patna 800 004
Chowk, Varanasi 221 001

Printed in India
by RP Jain at NAB Printing Unit,
A-44, Naraina Industrial Area, Phase I, New Delhi-110028
and published by JP Jain for Motilal Banarsidass Publishers (P) Ltd,
41 U.A. Bungalow Road, Jawahar Nagar, Delhi-110007

CONTENTS

INTRODUCTION 7

PREFACE 11

MEDITATIONS ON RAMAYANA AND TARAKA MANTRA 14

SRI RAMA MANTRA 20

Sage Valmiki 21
How the Ramayana Came to be Written 22
The Seven Books 22

RAMAYANA 25

BOOK I–BALA KANDA 27
- Dasharatha 27
- The Story of Risha-Shringa 27
- Birth of Rama 29
- Sage Vishwamitra 29
- Story of the Ganges 33
- Ahalya 36
- Sita 37
- Parashurama 41
- Parashurama and Sri Rama 42

BOOK II–AYODHYA KANDA 45
Manthara 50

BOOK III–ARANYA KANDA 92
Sage Sharabhanga 95
Sage Suteekshna 96
Sage Agastya 98
Shoorpanakha 101
Abduction of Sita 111
Jatayu 113
Story of Kabandha 120
Shabari 121
Pampa 125

BOOK IV–KISHKINDA KANDA 126

BOOK V–SUNDARA KANDA 154

BOOK VI–YUDDHA KANDA 176
Angada Sandhana 183

BOOK VII–UTTARA KANDA 203

SITA RAMA RAMA SITA RAM 207

RAMAYANA IN SONG 208

INTRODUCTION

By Sri H.H. Swami Vishnudevananda

The world is the stage on which the Lord played the part of Rama as the ideal son, brother, husband, step-son, and king. The story of Rama and Sita is verily the story of humanity. Sita, Rama's devoted consort, enacted the role of the dutiful, chaste wife who cared for nothing but her beloved Rama. Lakshmana was the perfect brother, and Bharata and Shatrughna were exemplary in their devotion to their step-brother, Rama.

The next main character, Hanuman, is the embodiment of a surrendered devotee—the pinnacle of Bhakti Yoga. The ten-headed Ravana, who plays the antagonistic role, symbolizes our ten senses (5 senses of knowledge and 5 senses of action). During the war, Rama beheads Ravana, which is characteristic of a *yogi* conquering the senses.

The characters in the Ramayana relate to our own human drama. The Ramayana teaches us a way of life. It shows how to have pure love among family members and toward society and gives us a method to control the ten senses and the mind for inner peace and spiritual bliss.

Life on this planet is short and man is immersed in emotional conflict in the form of attachments to the family, wife, children, etc. Identifying with Rama and Sita as manifestations of the Self in all is an easy method of pulling the mind away from its attachment to the various pleasure centers. In the ancient epic, the humble devotee, Hanuman, is the son of the wind god. The wind symbolizes sound. Without the wind, no sound is possible. Sound is the gross manifestation of mind and thought. In the transcendental state, sound waves manifest as thought waves. Thought waves in the gross material plane manifest as spoken language.

Singing the Lord's name on the gross plane can bring us to the transcendental level where sound manifests as pure energy. The name and form disintegrate in Pure Consciousness and ultimate peace is experienced. Repetition of the Lord's name in the form of *japa* or *kirtan* will bring the transcendental, blissful experience attained by the great devotees and saints like Bhakta Mira Bai, Tukaram, and in the present time, Sri Sant Keshavadas. Santji has followed the tradition of our great saints and devotees of the past and has now brought the story of the Ramayana for 20th century man. He has abridged this great epic without losing its meaning so that the ordinary, busy man can realize its truth.

As has been said by Lord Krishna to Sage Narada, "Naham Vasami Vaikunte Yoginam Hridayenacha; Madbhaktha Yatra Gayanti Tatra Tishtami Narada," meaning, "I always dwell where devotees sing the glory of My Name."

May this story of the Ramayana bring a new awakening to the turbulent hearts. Sant Keshavadas is the ideal devotee to bring this great epic to modern-day, busy man in the Kali Age.

Swami Vishnudevananda

SADGURU SANT KESHAVADAS

PREFACE

God incarnates age after age to restore *dharma*. Such incarnations are known as *avatars*. Sri Ramachandra is worshipped by the sages as the seventh incarnation of Lord Vishnu, and Sita, his spouse, is worshipped as Goddess Lakshmi's incarnation. All those who helped Rama or served him were the angels or *devatas*. This greatest story ever written is known as Ramayana. Originally, it was written by Sage Valmiki to the people of the earth, but it was very popular in the higher heirarchy in the heavens. We were told by Sage Valmiki that Brahma the Creator narrated this story to his son, Sage Narada, who made it popular in all upper heavens and then imparted it to Valmiki. Valmiki taught this to Rama's children, Lava and Kusha, who sang Ramayana to this world.

How Should One Read Ramayana

Ramayana is considered as a holy scripture. Rama lived the Vedic truths. One who wants to experience this Rama-consciousness or wants to obtain His *darshan* should bathe or shower, wear meditation clothes, and should do the *japa* or repetition of the 13-syllabled mantra, "Sri Rama Jaya Rama Jaya Jaya Rama" at least 108 times on the rosary, either orally, mentally, or both.

Then one should worship Sri Rama and Sita and the book of Ramayana by offering flowers and salutations. Filled with devotion to God, one should open this holy book and read it himself or to a few devotees and at the end of each Kanda or canto, he should wave the light before God and receive His grace. Before one begins reading Ramayana, it is important he should keep a wooden plank in the meditation room as a special seat to Lord Hanuman. He can keep an image or picture of Hanuman on the wooden plank; if not, he can just invoke Hanuman's presence by placing a coconut and lighting a candle and keeping them on or near the wooden plank. Hanuman has promised that wherever Sri Ramayana is read or sung, he will be present there invariably. None can see Rama without the blessings of Hanuman; therefore, to keep the wooden plank invoking his presence is important.

After the complete reading of Ramayana, one can feed the poor, offer clothes, or do some charity in the name of Rama. The benefits of reading or listening to the entire Ramayana, as per the scriptural injunctions given above, will be infinite. Forefathers are resurrected, sick are healed, and desires here and hereafter are fulfilled. More than anything, Cosmic Love is realized and the *darshan* of Rama is obtained. This is the traditional way of the sages and saints to read Ramayana.

Sri Rama and Hanuman blessed me to recite Ramayana 108 times to thousands of devotees in India. First, I read it for children in song form in Kannada language. Since that time, I had a deep wish to write it in English for the western devotees. By the blessings of the Lord, now that wish is fulfilled, and my heart is filled with peace. I have tried to write in these pages the wisdom of Sage Valmiki, Sant Tulasidas, Kamban, Narahari, Tyagaraja, and other saints. It is written in such a way that you could know the great Ramayana at a glance. By reading this, if it inspires you to go to the original Ramayana in Sanskrit, then my effort is rewarded.

I am very grateful to Sri H.H. Swami Vishnudevananda for his kind introduction. I must thank Sister Karuna for her special efforts in typing, reading, and editing this holy book. My thanks are due to Mrs. Swaran Batra, who read the manuscript with great patience and gave me valuable suggestions in editing. Thanks to Sister Lila, Sister Gayatri, and B.K. Geetha Pai, for their assistance. Ravidas, Master Shyam, Chandrashekhar, Umadevi, and Parabrahma, have given their total cooperation for this work. May God bless all these beautiful souls who have stood strong for Cosmic Religion. May the entire world be filled with joy and peace.

With Om and Prem,
Sant Keshavadas

July 25, 1976
Detroit, Michigan

MEDITATIONS ON RAMAYANA

Ramayana is not a mere story. It is the story we live every moment of our lives.

Dasharatha symbolizes the intellect that controls the ten senses. The three queens of Dasharatha are the three *gunas* known as *sattwa* (tranquility), *rajas* (activity), and *tamas* (inactivity). Vasishta and Vishwamitra are the *gurus* who guide the intellect. Rama is the Transcendental Self and Lakshmana, Bharata, and Shatrughna are the triple manifestations of God as immanent, God as indwelling spirit, and God as soul, respectively.

Manthara symbolizes the negative qualities that poison Kaikeyi, the *rajasic* mind. Demons and demonesses in Ramayana are the evil propensities in us. Ravana is the *rajasic* ego; Kumbhakarna is the *tamasic* ego; Vibhishana stands for *sattwic* ego. Rama's wife Sita is the Cosmic Energy (Kundalini) abducted by Ravana, the ego, for wrong use. So, through Hanuman, symbolizing *pranayama* or rhythmic breathing, you will find the location of Sita, the energy, and convey the news of Rama, the Self. Rama's destruction of Ravana and Kumbhakarna symbolizes the destruction of the *rajasic* and *tamasic* egos and the installation of Vibhishana symbolizes the establishment of *sattwa guna* and equanimity through Self-realization. Union of Rama and Sita is the union of Shakti with the eternal consciousness of the true Self. Rama's coronation symbolizes the Kingdom of Heaven on earth. This, in short, is the esoteric meaning of Ramayana.

TARAKA MANTRA

Sri Rama Jaya Rama Jaya Jaya Rama

This *mantra* is known as Trayodasha-Akshari or the 13-syllabled mantra. It is known as Taraka Mantra, which means the meditation on this *mantra* could take a man across the ocean of rebirth. Lord Shiva imparted this *mantra* to his spouse, Parvati, saying, "O Parvati, this Taraka Mantra is equivalent to a thousand names of Lord Vishnu."

In the *mantra* "Sri Rama Jaya Rama Jaya Jaya Rama," Sri stands for *shakti* or Sita. Ra symbolizes the fire that burns our *karma*. Ma represents water, which means the peace that passeth all understanding. Jaya means victory to the spirit over the flesh. Thus, the entire meaning of the *mantra* is "Victory to God with his *shakti*. Victory, victory to God."

Om stands for the word of God. It is the seed syllable

श्री राम जय राम जय जय राम
TARAKA MANTRA

or *bija mantra*. Therefore, Om is always prefixed to any *mantra*. Thus, the entire Taraka Mantra is sung as "Om Sri Rama Jaya Rama Jaya Jaya Rama."

In *yogic* parlance, Ra is the sun or solar energy, moving in *pingala nadi*, which is at the right side of the spine. It is masculine energy. Ma is the moon or lunar energy, moving in *ida nadi*, which is to the left of the spine. It is feminine energy. Thus, while you chant "Rama" again and again, it balances the masculine and feminine energy. Thus, you acquire balance of mind.

In devotional mysticism, it is described thus. When you chant "Ra", the mouth, which is the main gate of this body, opens wide, and all sins are thrown out. When you chant "Ma", your lips are locked and no sinful propensity can enter into you. Thus, by chanting Rama-nama, the devotee attains purity of mind and heart and God is realized in such a pure heart.

There are 72,000 *nadis* in the human body. Out of them, 108 *nadis* are in the heart. That is the location of God and soul. Therefore, 108 became a mystical number for doing *japa* or repetition of the holy *mantra*. *Japa* is the most powerful spiritual discipline in which the repetition of the holy *mantra*, along with *pranayama* or rhythmic breathing, is practiced.

In *japa*, there are three steps. *Vachika* or oral repetition is the first step. As the mind is entering into the meaning of the *mantra*, you reach the second stage known as *upamshu*, which means repeating the *mantra* where not even a whisper is heard while lips are moving. As you reach the third stage, it is purely mental repetition, known as *manasika japa*. Here the mind repeats the *mantra* uninterruptedly and ultimately is absorbed in God. Let a devotee practice these three steps of *japa* until he attains total absorption.

Rosary of beads or *japa mala* is inseparable from this *yogic* meditation. There should be 108 beads on a rosary which symbolizes 108 *nadis*. On some rosaries, the beads are only 54, in which case the devotee has to turn the rosary twice to make it 108. In one sitting the devotee must do the *japa* 108 times. Those who want to do intense *japa* should repeat the *mantra* 1008 times in one sitting.

After bathing or washing one's face, one should sit either in lotus posture or any easy posture where the chest, neck and the head are kept straight and steady for the energy to flow above through the spine. Holding the *japa mala* in the right hand, over the three fingers, middle, ring, and the little finger, one has to touch the bead by the thumb and the middle finger. After chanting the Holy Name, the bead is to be pushed and the same process should continue until one reaches the 108th bead or the last bead before the *meru* bead that stands separate from all of the other beads, that being transcendental. If one wants to continue the *japa*, one has to turn the rosary in such a way that he will not push the bead as he did before, but hold the bead by the thumb and the middle finger. Before repeating the *mantra*, one should inhale deeply and while exhaling, one has to chant the entire 13-syllabled *mantra* as mentioned above.

After the *japa*, one should salute the rosary and keep it either in a box or at the feet of God's image or symbol or hang the rosary on the wall. After 100,000 intense *japa*, one acquires healing power and then one has to touch the *meru* bead to the brow center of the patient. In the name of God, one should pray for healing. After such a healing, one should wash the rosary of *japa* again. Japa Yoga is the easiest, safest, and the surest way. It could be practiced by anybody at any time. According to the Bhagavad Gita, *japa* is the greatest of all sacrifices.

Taraka Mantra is the one *mantra* for the entire world. It has no restriction of age, sex, caste, color, creed, or country. It could be chanted by anyone at any time. This *mantra* solves the problems of lust and anger. It transforms the aggressive nature into a loving one. Sage

Valmiki, Sant Tulasidas, Samartha Ramadas, Bhabrachala Ramadas, Tyagaraja, Purandaradasa, are the greatest exponents of this *mantra*. Lord Shiva constantly meditates on Taraka Mantra and Lord Hanuman is the greatest devotee of Rama, who became the ever-living, diamond-bodied Master. In modern times, Mahatma Gandhi practiced Taraka Mantra and brought independence to India through his power of love and non-violence.

The holy scriptures declare another efficacious method, known as Likhita Japa, or writing this holy *mantra*. Have a few exercise books and a few pens reserved only for writing the holy *mantra*. If one writes everyday at least a page or more with deep devotion, gradually he will feel that his heart has become like a white paper, symbolizing purity, and he sees Ramanama written on it. In other words, he will realize that his soul remembers God uninterruptedly. One can take a pledge of writing 10,000 or 100,000 *mantras* per year with a deadline. Such an intense form of doing *japa* for obtaining certain results or God-realization, is known as *Turascharana Vidhi*, or the great discipline of realization. The devotee who has taken such a pledge will be maintaining *brahmacharya*, or celibacy, during those months of practice. He will fast now and then, eat little, talk little, sleep little. With intense longing to have the *darshan* of the beloved Lord, he repeats the Holy Name orally or mentally or both, or he writes the Holy Name after oral and mental chanting. One can practice all of these for quick results. Completing that number of *japa* within the deadline, the devotee performs a *puja* or worship of Rama and as a mark of completion of the vow, he will feed and clothe the poor or do some charity in God's name.

May everyone practice the Taraka Mantra Japa and attain peace and immortality.

Om Shanti, Shanti, Shanti

SRI RAMA MANTRA

Om Sri Ram Jai Ram Jai Jai Ram
Om Sri Ram Jai Ram Jai Jai Ram

(1) Chant the Name Divine, be calm
Sing the Name with all thy Prem
Make O mind, the Om thy home
Take thou shelter in God's Name
(Refrain)

(2) Sri Ram forgives, Sri Ram protects
Sri Ram bestows Eternal Peace
Sri Ram our Lord compassionate
On Ram, O mind, always meditate
(Refrain)

(3) Sri Ram showers His Supreme Grace
Sri Ram gives us Eternal Bliss
Sri Ram destroys all lust and sins
Sri Ram our Lord always loves us
(Refrain)

(4) Sri Ram mantra takes us across
It saved Kabir and Tulasidas
Lord Siva taught this to his spouse
This Taraka Mantra makes you Das
(Refrain)

Sage Valmiki

In a forest there lived a hunter named Rooksha. He was mercilessly looting and killing the people who passed through that forest. One day Narada, the Singing Saint, was passing through the forest. Hunter Rooksha chased him with his hatchet and raised it up to kill him. The Singing Saint went on singing the Holy Name of God. The hunter's raised hand and hatchet stood still, and however he tried, he could not move his hand. Seeing him miserable, the merciful Saint blessed him and the hunter threw his hatchet down and fell at the feet of Narada. He prayed him to forgive all his sins.

Narada asked him to chant the holy word, "Rama." His sinful tongue could not repeat that *mantra*. Then the Saint asked him to chant the word twistingly as "mara, mara." The hunter chanted *ma* and *ra*, "mara, mara," several times and as it took momentum, it fell into rhythm and he chanted "Rama, Rama." Narada initiated him and departed to his higher abode.

The hunter sat in lotus posture and meditated on the great vibration "Rama." This meditation led him to the door of Cosmic Consciousness. Settled in that highest state of consciousness, he sat for nearly twelve months without moving. An anthill completely covered his body. When his *guru* Narada came, he was very happy to see the enlightened disciple emerging out of that anthill.

In Sanskrit language "Valmika" means anthill. As he emerged from the anthill he was named "Valmiki."

Esoterically, this means each of us have this sagely consciousness in us. When our sins are washed away by meditation on the Holy Name imparted to us by our *guru*, then we emerge out of the anthill of this body and become saints.

How the Ramayana Came to be Written

Sage Narada narrated the story of Rama to his disciple Valmiki and inspired him to write and make it popular for the peace of humanity.

When Narada left for his abode, Valmiki went to the river Tamasa to bathe and meditate. There he saw a male bird bleeding, struck by the arrows of a fowler, and the female bird crying with agony and hovering around the body of the male bird. A rhythmic Sanskrit verse emerged from the lips of Sage Valmiki which was seemingly a curse to the fowler, but later he found that verse to be the beginning of Ramayana. Later, Sage Valmiki wrote the entire Ramayana in seven books containing 24,000 Sanskrit verses. This book became the national epic of India and is read in almost every home and in all temples. Ramayana is the guide for practical, happy life here and hereafter. Sri Rama is God incarnate, perfect man; and Sita is Goddess incarnate, perfect woman. Ramayana teaches divine love in practical life and is a guidebook for all married people, as it deals with happy marriage. Ramayana means "the way in which Rama walked" or "the path of perfection shown by Sri Rama." A daily reading of this book brings the blessings of wisdom, love, and peace. May Sri Rama and Sita bless all.

The Seven Books

Seven is a mystical number in all religious literature

of the world. God created the world in six days and on the seventh day He completed it and then rested. From that time onward the number seven was considered as a mystical number. Thus, you have seven rhythms of the famous *Gayatri Mantra*, seven upper spheres, seven lower regions, seven musical notes, seven days per week, and seven books of Ramayana.

The first book of Ramayana is known as *Bala Kanda* containing the divine birth of Rama, his childhood, and his marriage to Sita. The second book is *Ayodhya Kanda* which explains the preparations for Sri Rama's coronation and his exile to the forest. The third book is *Aranya Kanda* which narrates the forest life of Sri Rama and the kidnapping of Sita by demon Ravana. The fourth book is named *Kishkinda Kanda* which describes the meeting of Hanuman with Rama, the destruction of Vali, and the coronation of his younger brother Sugriva on the throne of Kishkinda. The fifth book is the beautiful canto named *Sundara Kanda* which explains the *lila* of Hanuman, who flies across the ocean, searches and finds Rama's spouse Sita, hands over Rama's ring to her, and returns to Rama. The sixth book is *Yuddha Kanda* which explains the battle between Rama's army and the demon army headed by Ravana. Rama destroys the demon Ravana and his army, installs Ravana's brother Vibhishana on the throne of Lanka, flies with Sita and his troop back to Ayodhya, and establishes *Rama Rajya* or the Kingdom of Heaven on earth. The seventh or last book of Ramayana known as *Uttara Kanda* explains the birth of Lava and Kusha to Sita in the hermitage of Valmiki, their coronation on the throne of Ayodhya, and Rama's final departure to his transcendental abode.

Whosoever reads this holy story of Sita, Rama, and Hanuman, will be blessed with longevity, prosperity, love, peace, happiness, and finally liberation.

Lord Rama, Sita, Lakshmana, and Hanuman

RAMAYANA

BOOK I

BALA KANDA

Dasharatha

In ancient times in India there lived a king named Dasharatha. He had three queens: Kausalya, Sumitra, and Kaikeyi. He ruled over a state named Kosala, the capital being the city of Ayodhya. He had eight efficient ministers in his cabinet. Brahma-rishi Vasishta was the head priest of the royal family who advised the king to rule righteously. The people were very happy and lived peacefully in his kingdom.

King Dasharatha ruled over Ayodhya for a long time. He had no children. That worried him and his queens very much. He approached Sage Vasishta for guidance. The sage advised him to perform a fire-sacrifice known as *Putra-Kameshti Yajna* which would bless him with children. To conduct this *yajna*, a great sage named Rishya-Shringa, among others, was invited. Vast arrangements were made on the bank of Sarayu River.

The Story of Rishya-Shringa

There lived a sage named Vibhandaka. By his *yogic* power he blessed a deer to give birth to a male baby. The boy was born with two horns on his head. The sage taught him the wisdom of God, and the strict disciplines of austerity and meditation. Born and brought up in the hermitage of the sage and living in the company of hermits, the boy had never seen a woman in his life. The power of his penance and meditation radiated all over the earth and people recognized him as a saint.

It so happened in a state called Anga there was a drought. The king, Romapada, came to know that if he invited Sage Rishya-Shringa to his state, the blessings of the sage would bring the rains. He sent a few beautiful maidens to tempt the *yogi* to visit Anga state.

When the saintly Rishya-Shringa came to pick a few flowers and fruits for the worship of God, the beautiful maidens began singing for him. Rishya-Shringa, who had never seen women before, began running away, thinking them to be some strange animals coming from another forest. The next day when he came to pick the flowers, those beautiful ladies surrounded him and enchanted his mind to go with them to bless Anga state.

Sage Rishya-Shringa went with them and no sooner the dust of his holy feet touched the soil of Anga state than the clouds gathered and rains poured, bringing peace and happiness to all. Such is the power of the presence of a saintly person! King Dasharatha invited this great Master to the fire-sacrifice. Sage Rishya-Shringa and Sage Vasishta performed the sacred *yajna*, assisted by many sages.

At the conclusion of the *yajna*, there arose a celestial person from the sacrificial altar. He was holding a golden vessel containing the essence of God. He offered this to King Dasharatha and asked him to distribute it to his three queens. They would be blessed by four children, the incarnations of God on earth. As the king and the queens saluted, the celestial person blessed them and disappeared.

Birth of Rama

King Dasharatha distributed the divine essence to his three queens. Half of the essence was given to the eldest queen, Kausalya. Out of the remaining half, one-quarter of the same was given to Kaikeyi. The remaining one-quarter was divided into two parts and Sumitra partook them separately. After some time all three queens conceived.

The most auspicious hour came. Celestials and sages rejoiced. Nature was calm. Flowers bloomed everywhere. Birds sang their joyful songs. There was spontaneous joy in everything.

Kausalya gave birth to Rama, Kaikeyi to Bharata, and Sumitra gave birth to the twins named Lakshmana and Shatrughna. They were all considered as Lord Vishnu's four manifestations, even though Rama was Vishnu's highest manifestation. Brahma-rishi Vasishta named them according to their qualities. Rama means "one who is absolutely beautiful in body, mind, and spirit." Bharata means "the fulfillment." Lakshmana means "of noble virtues." Shatrughna means "the destroyer of demons or enemies."

Lakshmana was closely attached to Rama and Shatrughna to Bharata. Therefore, people used to call the four brothers in the following order: Rama, Lakshmana, Bharata, and Shatrughna.

Sage Vasishta taught them the *Vedas, Upanishads*, and *Brahmasutras*. They were well-versed in many sciences including the science of archery and the art of warfare.

Sage Vishwamitra

Sage Vishwamitra was a seer of *Gayatri Mantra*. He knew that Rama was God incarnate. He had a special assignment in the *avatar* of Sri Rama. He came to

Ayodhya and announced himself at the gate. King Dasharatha welcomed him reverently, washed his holy feet, and offered an exalted seat. Vishwamitra told Dasharatha the purpose of his visit. "O king," the Sage said, "I have come to take Rama and Lakshmana with me to my Siddhashrama. There I am performing a great *yajna*, a fire-sacrifice, for universal peace. Tataka the demoness and her two sons, Mareecha and Subahu, are planning to destroy the fire-sacrifice. Rama has taken *avatar* for the destruction of the demons and the protection of the pious. Therefore, it is meet that he should go with me accompanied by Lakshmana."

Due to his deep attachment to Rama, King Dasharatha grieved for some time and said,"O Sage, Rama and Lakshmana are too tender for such a terrible task of destroying the powerful demons. Instead, I myself will come with my army to destroy the demons."

Sage Vishwamitra asked him to consult Sage Vasishta. Sage Vasishta blessed the king with the eye of knowledge to realize Rama's greatness. Dasharatha saw through the divine eye that Rama was none other than God.

Convinced of the greatness of Rama, Dasharatha happily sent Rama and Lakshmana with Sage Vishwamitra.

Seeing the panoramic view of nature, they walked until they reached the bank of Sarayu River. All three of them bathed in the pellucid waters of the holy river and did their evening *Gayatri* meditation. After meditating, they rested.

Early in the morning, Sage Vishwamitra arose and awoke Sri Rama with the following words, "Sri Rama, you have sanctified the womb of your mother, Kausalya. Look at the eastern horizon. The sun god is going to bless the whole world now and this is the time for morning meditation. Arise, O lion among men, and show the way to the world by your ideal!" Hearing this blessed word of the *guru*, Sri Rama arose, awoke Lakshmana, and both of them along with the *guru* bathed in the holy river and offered their morning oblations to the sun god.

As they were proceeding through a formidable forest, they heard a deafening noise that made the forest trees tremble. Holding both Rama and Lakshmana to his bosom, Vishwamitra told them of the demoness Tataka. "Rama, this is the forest where this demoness lives with her two sons, Subahu and Mareecha. They are creating havoc among the sages and saints, destroying the peace of the forest. Now they have decided to destroy the great fire-sacrifice which I have organized in our *ashrama*. As they are a threat to the society of holy men, it is proper that they should meet their death by your hand. Rama, there is no sin in slaying this demoness because the very purpose of your incarnation is the destruction of the demons and protection of the pious. Lo! Here she comes with her mouth agape like the cave of a mountain. Twang your bow, fix the sharp arrow, hit at her quickly, Rama, and send her to the abode of death."

Rama looked at Lakshmana and smiled. They were not afraid of the demoness at all, having learned the secret of chant arrows. Sri Rama discharged a very powerful arrow which severed the head of the terrible monstress from her trunk. To the joy of Vishwamitra, the celestials showered flowers and trumpets were sounded in honor of Sri Rama, who relieved the earth of its burden by the destruction of Tataka.

Sri Rama and Lakshmana came to Siddhashrama along with Vishwamitra. They were welcomed by a host of sages who had been meditating years and years for the *darshan* or the vision of Rama. They chanted the *Vedic mantras* and received them with great devotion. The next day, the fire-sacrifice for universal peace began under the direction of Vishwamitra. Sage Vishwamitra alarmed Rama and Lakshmana of the disturbance which might come at any time from the two demon sons of Tataka, Subahu and Mareecha. Accordingly, Rama and Lakshmana stood back to back, holding their bow and arrow ready to protect the sages and their fire-sacrifice from the demons.

As expected, Subahu and Mareecha began to pour blood and wine into the sacrificial altar to make it unholy. They roared like thunder and appeared as different animals to drive away the sagely assembly. It took no time for Sri Rama and Lakshmana to fix them. Even as the mist is lifted before the scorching rays of the sun, the magic of the demons and their illusory appearances came to an end by the powerful arrows discharged by Rama. When demon Subahu attempted to kill Rama, Rama's fire arrow reduced him to ashes instantaneously.

Demon Mareecha grieved at the loss of his brother and wanted to retaliate. When he showered thousands of arrows on Rama and Lakshmana like a swarm of humming bees, Rama's arrows covered all four directions, dispelling the illusory power of the demon. Turning to his younger brother, Rama said, "Lakshmana, look at this interesting arrow. Just a few hours ago Sage Vishwamitra taught the secret *mantra* of how to discharge this arrow over the demon. Now you can see the power of this arrow which will not kill the demon Mareecha but will toss him across the seven seas." Saying thus, Sri Rama hit the arrow at the demon, who was carried away by the power of the arrow across the seven oceans, like a withered leaf by the tempestuous wind. Demon Mareecha fell in a forest in the country called Lanka where he built his *ashram* and meditated on Rama out of fear. Fear of God is the beginning of knowledge.

After the successful completion of the *yajna*, Sage Vishwamitra decided to take Sri Rama and Lakshmana to the city of Mithila. Sages blessed Sri Rama and Lakshmana and bid a grand farewell to them.

On the way to Mithila, Sage Vishwamitra narrated various stories. When Rama and Lakshmana saw the holy river Ganges, they were eager to know how the celestial river came to the earth. Thereby Vishwamitra narrated the story of the descent of the Ganges.

Story of the Ganges

"Hear, O beloved Rama and Lakshmana, in the same Solar dynasty in which you were born, in ancient times, there was a king named Bhagiratha. For a long time after his married life he had no children. He consulted Sage Vasishta whether there was any curse upon the family causing such misery of having no children. The Sage said, 'O King, it is definitely a curse and the story behind the curse is as follows. There was a king named Sagara. When he was performing a horse-sacrifice, Indra, the head of the angels, stole away his horse and hid it in the nether regions near the hermitage of a *yogi* named Kapila. Indra did this out of fear that King Sagara may dethrone him by the power which he might receive by the performance of the horse-sacrifice. King Sagara was utterly depressed at the disappearance of the celestial horse, without which he could not perform the sacrifice. His sixty thousand sons (this may be interpreted as his subjects, whom he treated as sons) went in search of the horse until finally they made their way to the nether regions where they found the horse. But out of arrogance they insulted Sage Kapila by abusing him for stealing the horse. Sage Kapila reduced all sixty thousand people to ashes by uttering a curse. King Sagara was agonized to hear of this catastrophe and sought the advice of sages. They advised him to bring the holy Ganges from heaven to the earth and then to the nether regions, making her flow over the ashes of the sixty thousand people. This act alone would bring salvation to their souls. Then the curse of the sage would be lifted and progeny would continue.

" 'King Sagara's son Amshumanta, however, brought the horse back and King Sagara performed the *yajna* successfully. Sagara tried his best to bring the Ganges on earth but he could not do it. Having ruled for a number of years, he ascended to heaven. King Amshumanta and his son, Dilipa, tried their utmost to bring the celestial river to the earth. They were also unsuccessful in their attempt. 'O Bhagiratha,' Sage Vasishta concluded, 'if you could bring the holy river Ganges to the earth and nether regions, and bring peace to those souls, that blessing will bring children to your family.'

"O Rama," Sage Vishwamitra continued, "King Bhagiratha took a pledge to bring Mother Ganges to earth, take her to the nether regions, and make her flow over the ashes of the sixty thousand sons of Sagara. Bhagiratha went to the Himalayas and began performing rigorous *tapasya* or austerity. Creator Brahma was pleased, seeing his austere penance, and appeared to him. 'O Bhagiratha,' said the creator, 'I am pleased with you. Ask any boon you want.' Bhagiratha made obeisance to the creator and said, 'My Lord, my only desire is to bring the celestial river Ganges to flow on earth and in nether regions. Please send her down from heaven.' The creator said, 'Bhagiratha, I shall send the holy Ganges down to earth but you have to pray to Lord Shiva, who alone can stand the mighty gush of the Ganges.' Saying thus, the creator Brahma disappeared.

"Bhagiratha was not discouraged. Restraining his breath, fixing his gaze in the mid of the brows, with uplifted arms, the strongwilled Bhagiratha meditated on Lord Shiva for a number of years. A smoke emerged from the crown of the head of that great king, scorching the three worlds. Such was the power of his austerity. Angels appealed to Lord Shiva to bless the king, lest his power shall burn the whole world. Lord Shiva, pleased with the devotion of Bhagiratha, appeared to him. 'Arise, O great king, and ask for the boon of your choice,' said the Lord. Bhagiratha prayed the Lord to channel the Ganges smoothly to the earth from heaven and bless his efforts with success. Lord Shiva agreed and stood there asking the king to invoke the Ganges.

"At the insistence of Creator Brahma and prayers of Bhagiratha, the mighty Ganges river gushed forth. To curb her ego, Lord Shiva stopped her torrential pour by arresting her in his matted locks. King Bhagiratha felt very sad that so much of his effort was wasted, but he never gave up. He once again invoked Lord Shiva's blessings by the following prayer. 'O, Mahadeva! You are the God of all the gods. You are the bestower of the great boons. You are easily attained through devotion. When a child named Upamanyu approached you for milk, you gave him the ocean of milk. O compassionate Shiva, I see your transcendental form with crescent moon, and Mother Ganges hiding in your matted locks. O three-eyed Lord, destroyer of death, be pleased with me and send Mother Ganges smoothly to earth.' Lord Shiva, pleased with the prayer of Bhagiratha, sent the Ganges to the earth. Despite curbing her ego, still the torrential pour of the Ganges shook the earth and she split into seven streams. One major stream, at the prayer of Bhagiratha, followed him wherever he went. Gods showered flowers from heaven on Bhagiratha who, for the first time, brought the celestial river which had sprung from the toe of Vishnu, the Heavenly Father. They called her now Bhagirathi, which means the daughter of Bhagiratha. Still the difficulties were not over. The river, on her way, washed away the hermitage of a sage named Jahnu. He was very angry and by the power of his austerity, squeezed the Ganges in the cavity of his palm and drank the whole river. Bhagiratha cried bitterly that all his efforts went ineffectual. Washing the feet of the master with his tears, he requested the sage to send the river back. It is said Sage Jahnu took mercy on Bhagiratha and sent her back through his ear. Thereby, the gods called the river Jahnavi, which means the daughter of Sage Jahnu.

"Bhagiratha requested Mother Ganges to follow him to the nether regions, to which she agreed. They went to the nether regions or Patala, where he made her flow over the ashes of the sixty thousand sons of Sagara. By the touch of the holy river, the souls of Sagara's sons reached heaven and found peace."

Even today this story inspires millions of people by giving the following message: Have a noble idea, don't mind failures, and stop not till the goal is reached. One effort more and success shall be yours. Bhagiratha is the ideal of all human efforts. Mother Ganges flows in heaven, earth, and nether regions and therefore is considered holy among all the rivers. Symbolically it is the river of life.

Ahalya

Sri Rama heard a prayer from a distance. He told Lakshmana and Vishwamitra that some soul was waiting for his blessing. All of them went in that direction and Rama saw a huge rock. Full of compassion, he touched the rock with his holy feet. No sooner the pollen of his holy feet touched the rock than the rock melted and a celestial lady arose and bent like a creeper at the feet of the Lord. She glorified Sri Rama thus, "My Lord, Indra the head of the angels, disguised as my husband Sage Gautama, touched me, and my husband angrily uttered a curse on me and reduced me to this rock state. By my prayers he softened the curse, telling me I should meditate until God Vishnu incarnates as Rama and comes to me. It is by the touch of the dust of his holy feet I will be restored to my original pure body. Sri Rama, I was waiting for your arrival for many years and today you blessed me with your *darshan*. Sri Rama, you have come to resurrect the fallen souls. You are Lord Vishnu walking on earth. O Bhagavan, bless me with pure devotion to your lotus feet." Sri Rama blessed Ahalya with pure *bhakti*. Celestials sang the praise of the Lord and Vishwamitra sang benediction. Sage Gautama was very happy to receive his wife and both of them saluted Sri Rama again.

Sri Rama continued his journey along with Lakshmana and Vishwamitra toward the city of Mithila. The message of the above story is that Ahalya represents our Pure Consciousness. Due to ego and sinful propensities, our heart becomes like a rock in which this Pure Consciousness remains unmanifested. It takes a long time to realize this Pure Consciousness. It is through austerity and meditation we invoke Sri Rama, the Heavenly Father, and the touch of the divine frees this bound consciousness and we are restored to our pristine purity.

Sita

King Janaka had no children. He wanted to perform a great fire-sacrifice. According to the scriptural injunctions he had to plow a piece of land with a golden furrow. As he was plowing, he came across a thousand-petalled lotus in which he found a transcendental baby girl crying, "Om, Om." Sita, in Sanskrit, means furrow. As she was discovered while plowing, she was named Sita (pronounced as Seeta). Janaka and his kingdom rejoiced at the manifestation of the Universal Power of God in the form of that divine child. Sages declared her to be the *avatar* of Lakshmi, the goddess of prosperity and spouse of Vishnu. Sita used to hear the divine discourses given by great Masters at the spiritual assembly in her father's court. She became well-versed in *Vedas* and *Upanishads*. When she was five years of age a miracle happened. King Janaka saw Sita playing with the time-honored, mighty bow of Shiva called Sunabha. She was lifting and twanging the bow which was impossible even for thousands of strong soldiers. This convinced King Janaka and his people that Sita was *Vishnu Shakti* or the power of Vishnu. This episode is described in Ananda Ramayana. King Janaka organized Sita's marriage and the traditional *swayamvara* or choosing one's husband among the gathered suitors. The stipulation was, those who want to marry Sita should lift, string, and fix the arrow to the mighty Shiva bow. As Sita's beauty and fame had reached all over, many princes arrived to try to lift the Shiva bow and marry her.

Sage Vishwamitra brought Sri Rama and Lakshmana with him and introduced them to King Janaka. King Janaka was very happy to meet them. They took their seats along with Sage Vishwamitra in the assembly of the sages, because they were in hermit's attire. Shiva's bow was brought to the court on an eight-wheeled steel chariot, pushed by five thousand military soldiers. Seeing this, many of the princes fainted. Now King Janaka brought his beautiful daughter, Sita, who was shining like lightning, illumining the whole court. King Janaka's brother, Kushadhvaja, had three daughters named Mandavi, Urmila, and Shrutakirti. They were also brought to sit with Sita. The eyes of the whole audience were transfixed by the full moon-like faces of the princesses. King Janaka announced that whosoever lifts the Shiva bow and strings it shall be his son-in-law. For all others, his daughter will be like their mother.

Hearing these words, one by one the princes began trying their luck. As they failed to lift the bow, on their return to their seats, they were mocked by the ladies.

Suddenly a tumultuous noise was heard. Earth began quaking. People were terrified. In minutes they found that it was the ten-headed demon, Ravana, who arrived there on his special plane named Pushpaka Vimana. Seeing the demon, all were frightened. He came and announced that he was going to lift the Shiva bow and marry Sita. Saying thus, he came near the Shiva bow and tried to lift it. Using all twenty arms, the ten-headed demon shook the bow and began pushing it and pulling it. The earth began rocking like a cradle as he struggled to lift the bow. The mighty demon, after lifting the bow, tried to string it; but the weighty Shiva bow fell on his bosom and the demon sank with its weight on him, vomiting blood. Sages said he would have died instantaneously but for his *karma* written on his forehead. King Janaka's five thousand men took the bow away from his body. The defaced Ravana challenged Janaka, "When the right time comes, I shall carry away your beautiful daughter Sita." Saying thus, he flew back to Lanka in his aerial car.

Now the question came, who would be able to lift Shiva's bow? King Janaka's minister announced again that any daring prince could come forward and try to lift the bow. Seeing the time opportune, Sage Vishwamitra looked at Rama and said, "Sri Rama, the time has come for you to manifest your divine glory. Lift and string the bow and marry Sita."

Hearing the words of the *guru*, Sri Rama reverentially bowed to him and stood up. The beaming light of his countenance illumined the entire hall. Even as the full moon emerging from the ocean of milk while it was churned, so Rama's face shone as he stood up. As the blue-bodied Rama walked toward the Shiva bow, his toenails were shining like the crescent moon and every limb was radiating peace and love, bringing joy to everybody. The eternal youth of the Lord, combined with the symmetrical limbs of his body, attracted the eyes, mind, and heart of the whole gathering. The angels and celestials praised Sri Rama, seeing in him Lord Vishnu. Realized sages saw in him the Transcendental Godhead. For other princes he was seen as God incarnate. For all women he was seen as a personification of transcendental beauty and love. Rama moved toward the bow majestically like a young elephant. Sita's friends were inspired at the sight of Rama and came running to

Sita. They whispered in her ear, "Sita, Sita, the eyes are useless if they cannot feast on the beauty of Rama. No man has ever walked over the earth with such peace, love, and beauty. He definitely must be God incarnate." Sita, whose eyes were fixed on the ground out of shyness, just lifted her eyes once and gazed at the full moon-like face of Sri Rama. Now, however she tried, she couldn't move her eyes away from Sri Rama. All she could do was to close her eyes for a moment and meditate on Rama. She also prayed to Parvati, the spouse of Shiva, to ask Shiva to lighten the bow.

Rama stood near the bow and just turned his face toward Guru Vishwamitra and by an eye signal asked the *guru* what he should do. Sage Vishwamitra answered with his eyes to lift and snap the bow into two. With unwinking eyes, thousands of princes and ladies gazed when Sri Rama lifted that mighty Shiva bow as playfully as an elephant would lift a sugarcane. The Divine Lord bent the bow to string it and during the process of stringing, the bow snapped into two with a tumultuous noise like a clap of thunder. Celestial nymphs danced above the clouds and from the heavens fell a shower of flowers. King Janaka's joy knew no bounds. Sage Vishwamitra's face beamed with a divine smile. Lakshmana was very happy. Sita could not hold her joy. All were blissful. At the instance of her father Janaka, Sita rose from her seat and threw the garland around the neck of Sri Rama. Trumpets sounded, drums and kettledrums were played, clarinets and flutes were sounded, and people hailed them, "Sita Rama Ki Jai."

King Janaka sent special messengers to the court of King Dasharatha, inviting him to the marriage ceremony. Dasharatha, with his queens and relatives, arrived at King Janaka's palace. All the details of the ceremony were conducted by the priests and the sages according to the scriptural injunction. Finally, placing the hand of Sita in the hand of Sri Rama, King Janaka said these words,

"Rama, I hand over my daughter Sita as your partner in life for both of you to practice *dharma*. It is with this spirit you receive her hand in marriage. May all good attend on you both. Hold her hand now as your wife. She will be chaste in thought, word, and deed, and follow you even as a shadow follows a man. Sri Rama, receive Sita in that spirit."

This was the greatest marriage the world would ever see. As Dasharatha's other two sons, named Bharata and Shatrughna, had also arrived with the king, Janaka decided to marry all of them to his brother's daughters. All sages agreed. Accordingly, Bharata was married to Mandavi, Lakshmana to Urmila, and Shatrughna to Shrutakirti.

Parashurama

Sage Parashurama was the son of Sage Jamadagni. He was the sixth incarnation of Lord Vishnu. As his sagely father was killed by an arrogant king named Kartaveerya, Parashurama challenged the king in a battle and killed him. As India of those days was filled with demonic kings, it is said Parashurama went around India twenty-one times and destroyed those kings. As the main purpose of his *avatar* was to destroy the demons and protect the good, when accomplished, Parashurama thought of retiring to the Himalayas, for according to divine plan, he had to be the ever-living Master of the Himalayas.

Parashurama's *avatar* was in *Kritayuga* or the Golden Age. By the time Lord Vishnu's higher manifestation appeared as Sri Rama, Parashurama decided to hand over the future responsibility to his counterpart, Sri Rama, so the entire world would know that Rama is the seventh *avatar* of Vishnu. This clearly explains, an *avatar* alone is able to recognize another *avatar*. The devotees of God may feel one is an *avatar* though they cannot explain how or why.

After Rama's marriage to Sita, his three brothers married the three daughters of Janaka's brother, as explained earlier. Bharata's maternal uncle took Bharata and his wife Mandavi, and Shatrughna and his wife Shrutakirti, to his distant city called Girivrajapura. Rama and Lakshmana, with their wives and parents, started the journey back to Ayodhya. King Janaka gave his daughters many rich presents and servants and then took leave of them. Sage Vishwamitra blessed all of them and left for the Himalayas.

Parashurama and Sri Rama

As Sri Rama and his people were marching toward the city of Ayodhya, a tempestuous wind arose, overturning trees and rocks, and they saw the most powerful Sage Parashurama (Rama with a hatchet) arriving there. Dasharatha saw his end had come near. He had escaped from the hatchet of Parashurama twenty-one times, by marrying each time Parashurama came around the country destroying warrior class people. It was Parashurama's vow that whichever warrior sat for penance or was marrying at the time of his arrival would not be killed. Every time Parashurama came, Dasharatha was engaged in marriage and Janaka was doing penance. Thus, they were the only two kings who were left without being killed. Sri Rama consoled his father by saying, "Father, I shall meet the challenge of Parashurama."

An *avatar* should act like a human being without losing his identity with the Self. If he always acts in his divine way, then human beings cannot understand him.

That is why they say God descends on earth for the ascent of man. Therefore, the whole conversation between Parashurama and Rama is a drama of God and should not be misunderstood as one God to be fighting with the other.

Parashurama said, "O Rama, son of Dasharatha, do not be puffed up with pride that you have broken the mighty Shiva bow. I have come here to test your strength by bringing Lord Vishnu's bow. If you string this bow, then alone can I call you an extraordinary person." Hearing these words, Sri Rama of great prowess took Vishnu's bow away from Parashurama's hands. Sri Rama bent it playfully and fixed an arrow to it and said, "O Sage Parashurama, the warrior class people always revere men of wisdom like you. As I have taken the bow of Vishnu away from you, it will be mine. For the future destruction of the demons, I shall use this bow." While Rama was speaking these words, a great light emerged from Parashurama which merged in Sri Rama and Sri Rama was shining like thousands of suns. To see this rare phenomenon, the celestials, angels, semigods, and demigods, gathered in large numbers above and showered flowers on Sri Rama. This light coming from Parashurama to Rama was the symbolic transfer of power. Parashurama glorified Sri Rama, thus, "O Ramachandra, my mission on earth is finished. Vishnu's bow which you have in your possession shall be used for the destruction of demon Ravana and his brother Kumbhakarna, for which you have taken *avatar*. May the possession of this bow bring you all glory and may you restore *dharma* on earth. Now I shall withdraw to the Himalayas."

Saying thus, Parashurama disappeared to the Himalayas. Dasharatha embraced his son Rama with great joy. Thereupon, Rama with his people returned to Ayodhya. The people of Ayodhya made vast arrangements to receive Sri Rama and Lakshmana and with great pomp and glory they entered the city. They lived very happily in the beautiful palace of Dasharatha, delighting their parents and citizens of Ayodhya. Bharata and Shatrughna lived with their wives, their uncle, and grandfather in the distant city of Girivrajapura. Rama and Sita, the ideal of happy marriage, lived with great love and peace. When Heavenly Father Vishnu and Universal Mother Lakshmi have taken *avatar* as Rama and Sita, what other example does one need in this world to lead a happy married life?

Here ends the first book of Ramayana known as *Bala Kanda*.

BOOK II

AYODHYA KANDA

Sri Rama assisted his father in ruling over the kingdom and brought joy and peace to his subjects. Sri Rama was respected by everybody as a perfect man on earth. He was perfect in every limb, thought, word, and deed. He was the most beautiful among men and the most powerful. He was compassionate, truthful, benevolent, and well-disciplined. Rama spoke to the purpose and his words were like nectar to the hearers. He never hurt anyone in thought, word, or deed. Everyone was drawn toward him automatically like the needles toward the magnet. Rama was *Satya-sankalpa* which means true to his words. He was selfless, always thinking and acting toward the welfare of humanity. Whosoever develops this discipline of *Satya-sankalpa*, attains the power of accomplishing his goal of bringing peace to humanity. Whatever he thinks, being the truth, happens in cosmic order. Whatever he speaks becomes true by the virtue of his abiding in truth. Whatever he does brings infinite results for millions of years to come as an ideal to be followed by the entire humanity.

Sri Rama upheld the scriptures and *dharma* beyond

everything. He practiced *Gayatri* meditation according to the *Vedas*. As an incarnation of God, of course, he need not practice any meditation at all. But as is the standard shown by an ideal man, the generality of men follow his path. To show the way, the truth, and life, Sri Rama upheld the law and the prophets.

Sri Rama practiced *Ekapatnivrita* which means "a vow of seeing your wife in only one woman throughout life." It implies seeing all other women as one's own sisters or mothers. Seemingly simple, this vow is the most difficult of all to practice. Not even in dream to think of another woman, other than Sita, was the vow of Rama. It was equally true Sita practiced the same, seeing all men, other than Rama, as her children or brothers.

Just this practice of one virtue alone is enough to reach Godliness and there is no wonder that people worship Rama and Sita as the *avatar* of Vishnu and Lakshmi.

Rama was also known for his vow of *Ekavachana* which means "a man of one word." In other words, he would carry out his word of promise even at the cost of his life. He was well-known for his prowess so people called him *Ekabana* or "a man of one arrow," which means Rama's arrow shall never return unless it accomplishes its work. Thus, Rama was revered by all the subjects as a man of one word, one arrow, and one wife. Rama respected everyone, loved everyone, and was merciful toward all, but at the same time he was a man of strict discipline, of stern rule, and a terror to the demons. He was an ideal son, ideal husband, ideal brother, and an ideal king. He was practical in every aspect of life. He knew the *Vedas, Upanishads, Puranas*, and all the scriptures. He was the fulfillment of all scriptures and divine virtues. He was the jewel among men and the greatest of all the kings of Solar races.

Sita was an embodiment of chastity. She was the personification of all divine virtues. In many virtues she excelled Sri Rama. She served Rama in every capacity. All people saw a pure Divine Mother in her. Lakshmana served Rama not only as his elder brother but also as God.

King Dasharatha had a bad dream one night. He saw his body without his head. Later, he found through the astrologers that the dream was a warning that his death was nearing. So King Dasharatha decided to install Rama as regent. He called an immediate meeting of his cabinet and the important heads of various offices of his country. As it was an urgent meeting, he could not send an invitation to Bharata and Shatrughna, who were living in a very distant city. Sitting in the midst of that great assembly, King Dasharatha addressed them thus, "O men of wisdom, I have ruled over this country for a long period. I do not remember a single instance of transgressing *dharma* consciously or unconsciously. I have tried to rule my kingdom as it was ruled by my forefathers. I have lived long. Now I see the evening of my life approaching fast. I want to see, as according to this tradition of the Solar dynasty, my eldest son Rama take over the responsibility as the future king of Ayodhya. I need not boast over the qualities of my son Rama. It is all very well-known to you. Rama excels me in many qualities and has already endeared himself to all of you. He has pledged to promote the welfare of his people, and his wisdom is that of the preceptor of celestials named Brihaspati. He is firm in his decisions and I am sure he will rule over the dominion a thousand times better than I have. As my death is fast approaching, I would like to install Sri Rama on my throne without any more delay. Once he is coronated, I can reach the Kingdom of Heaven without any anxiety. I have already given serious thought to this matter. I do not see any transgression from *dharma* in this noble decision. But I would appreciate it if anyone in this assembly has any difference of opinion regarding this decision of mine." Saying thus, the king became silent. The whole assembly with one voice declared their consent to the king's decision. They said, "O great king, under your rule we were all very happy. Under the rule of Rama, we are sure we will be happier. We can't wait to see Sri Rama riding on the celestial elephant led in procession. It is our cherished desire to see Rama sitting under the shade of the white umbrella bearing the insignia of royalty."

Brahma-rishi Vasishta selected the auspicious moment to be the ascent of Pushya star the very next day. King Dasharatha handed over the responsibility to Sage Vasishta and Vamadeva to make all the preparations for Rama's coronation. The king said, "It is spring. All the trees are decked with flowers. Let my son Rama be installed tomorrow as the moment is auspicious."

The king also commanded his minister, Sumantra, to make all preparations for the great ceremony. The news was spread everywhere, and as notice was short, people were busy preparing for the ceremony by decorating their houses and the city. All were inspired and happy that their beloved Rama was going to be installed the very next day. They were chanting the Holy Name of Rama and working very hard to receive Rama the next day when he would come in a great procession. Palaces and all the gates of the city were decorated. Princes and sages were invited from different states. All worship materials such as garlands, perfumes, and flowers were gathered, and large amounts of food were prepared. When Sage Vasishta and Vamadeva told the king that almost all preparations were completed, the king sent Sumantra to bring Sri Rama to him. When Rama came, his beaming countenance brought peace to Dasharatha. Reverentially, he touched the feet of his father and stood with joined palms. Dasharatha lifted him, embraced him, and felt very happy. The king made Sri Rama sit comfortably on a beautiful seat and told him of his noble decision. He said, "Oh my son Rama, there is none equal to you in all the three worlds. I am the happiest of all fathers to have such a God-like son. Even as a man feels happy seeing his reflection in the mirror, similarly, I see myself in you and you shall bring a great name to this Solar dynasty. I know you have no desire for any position other than for the maintenance of world order and for the establishment of *dharma*. O noble son, accept the throne of Ayodhya and rule over the people of this great kingdom righteously. I know I need not give any advice to you as you are the embodiment of all virtues; still, as a father and an experienced king, I give this advice to you. My son, win the heart of the people with your affection, caring for their welfare. Rule over this kingdom with your mind perfectly under control."

Sri Rama, who knew what was going to happen, was neither jubilant at these glad tidings, nor sad; even-minded as he was, he obeyed his father and made his obeisance. Thereafter, he left for his palace to meditate with Sita throughout the night, as per the instruction of Sage Vasishta. On his way he visited his mother Kausalya at her palace. He conveyed the joyful news to his mother by saying, "O beloved mother, father wants to install me tomorrow on the throne of Ayodhya. At the advice of Sage Vasishta I am fasting and meditating with Sita at my palace. Bless me." Kausalya blessed her beloved son Sri Rama and offered her prayers to the family deity to crown the occasion with success. Sri Rama assured his brother Lakshmana of his eternal love and said to him, "O brother Lakshmana, assist me in ruling the kingdom of Ayodhya. With you alone, all the pleasures of the empire become meaningful to me." Thereafter, Rama saluted his mother Kausalya, step-mother Sumitra, and left for his palace.

Sri Ramachandra and Sita, after bathing, began worshipping the family deity. After the worship, both of them meditated awhile. They decided to fast and observe silence throughout the night.

Manthara

Queen Kaikeyi's maidservant, Manthara, was a hunchbacked woman. As she was a crooked baby when she was born, her parents left her in a forest. Kaikeyi's father, who went to that forest for hunting, saw the forlorn child, took pity on it, picked it up and brought it to his palace. Later, she was appointed by the king to take care of his daughter, Kaikeyi. From that day onward, she served Kaikeyi with all her heart. When Kaikeyi married Dasharatha, she accompanied Kaikeyi to the royal palace of Dasharatha and attended Kaikeyi as her servant. She was hated by all but Kaikeyi for her evil vibrations. Manthara loved Kaikeyi and her son Bharata with all her heart.

While climbing her balcony, the hunchbacked Manthara saw the decoration of Ayodhya city. She saw crowds of people fixing banners to the terraces of their homes and chanting Rama's name. She also saw a priest chanting the *Vedas* and people playing their musical instruments. The entire city was bright with lights and people were extremely busy decorating the important streets. She inquired of one of the maidservants the reason for such rejoicing. The maidservant told her Sri Rama would be coronated as regent by King Dasharatha the next day. Hearing these words, the crooked mind of the hunchbacked one was very depressed, and she descended from the balcony in a hurry and ran posthaste to her queen, Kaikeyi. Knocking at the door of her bedchamber, she awoke Kaikeyi, saying, "Kaikeyi, Kaikeyi, when the world outside is deluged, how happily you are sleeping. Wake up. Know you not that a great disaster is waiting for you? Oh, we are gone. Oh, you will be exiled. Oh, your son Bharata may have to beg in the streets of Ayodhya or, who knows, he may be banished from his own country."

Hearing the confusing words of Manthara, Kaikeyi

arose from her bed, opened the door, and called Manthara in. She asked Manthara the cause of her distressing words. The cunning Manthara began excreting the venom of her jealousy toward Rama as she spoke to Kaikeyi. She said, "Oh my dear queen of Ayodhya, you are deceived by your own people. Ignorant as you are about the situation, you are deluded to think your position to be safe. I have very bad news for you. Rama, the son of Kausalya, shall be installed on the throne of Ayodhya tomorrow by your husband, King Dasharatha. Thereafter, the eldest queen, Kausalya, will become the queen mother and acquire all powers. She was waiting to retaliate you, because the king loves you so much. The king has also deceived you by not telling you of his decision. He has deceived your son Bharata as well by not inviting him or sending him any information about Rama's coronation. Everything is arranged secretly and your destruction is near. O Kaikeyi, I am worried for you and also about the fate of dear Bharata. I wanted to kill myself instead of seeing you and Bharata suffering endlessly. O Kaikeyi, how happily you are sleeping without knowing the danger."

Hearing the news of Sri Rama's coronation, Kaikeyi was beside herself with joy. She ran into her treasury room and brought with her precious ornaments. Presenting them to Manthara, Kaikeyi said, "O Manthara, never in my life was I as happy as I am today at this exceedingly good news. Rama is dearer to me than my own son Bharata. I see no difference between them, and Bharata will be very happy at hearing this news. Perhaps the king had no time in conveying this news to me or sending a messenger to Bharata, who is living in a distant city. It is the tradition of the Solar race to proclaim the eldest son as the prince regent of the kingdom. Thank you for this nectarian news. I will give you many more presents of your choice. Do not be confused. Be at peace."

Hearing these words of Kaikeyi, Manthara began

hissing like a cobra and she threw away the presents given by Kaikeyi, saying, "O beloved queen, wonderful is your love for Rama. How compassionate you are! I have never seen a mother who would see the destruction of her own son and rejoice at other's children. O good lady, I want to tell you all that glitters is not gold. Rama shows outwardly all politeness; inwardly, he is just waiting for an opportunity to retaliate on his brother. He has been loving you only to acquire the kingdom. Once he is installed on the throne, he may banish you from the country. Know it for certain, I am the only one who cares for your welfare. If you doubt me, just give me permission to go away from here. I would like to fling myself into a river or throw myself down from a mountain or plunge into the fire to put an end to my life. O Kaikeyi, be kind enough to give me a cup of poison so that I may not live to see the suffering of you and Bharata. O noble lady, can't you understand this much? Can Dasharatha organize a coronation ceremony throughout the night without mentioning it even to his own wife? If your husband, King Dasharatha, had good intentions, then why didn't he invite Bharata and Shatrughna for a great occasion as this? His evil intentions are made clear by these two factors. Whether you believe me or not, Rama's coronation will mean doom for both you and Bharata."

The evil words of Manthara slowly poisoned the mind of Kaikeyi. Such is the power of evil company! Kaikeyi embraced Manthara and made her sit comfortably. She requested her to advise her clearly what she should do. She said, "O Manthara, I am sorry for paining your compassionate heart. I know you are my true well-wisher. You have tenderly taken care of me from childhood. You have brought up my son Bharata, too. I see very clearly the evil intentions of the king. I do seek your valuable advice to deal with this situation."

Manthara said, "My dear Kaikeyi, I am happy you

trust me. You know that long ago King Dasharatha gave you two boons of your choice. You have treasured them all these years without asking him what you desired. Now is the time to ask for those two boons. Any time now your husband may come. Listen carefully. I shall organize the room and tell you how you should look. When he comes to you and asks what you want, do not answer. Just go on crying and crying until the old dotard king swears by the name of Rama, whom he loves so much, and then he will give you whatever you want. O good lady, then you should be very clear in reminding him of the two boons which he gave you long ago. You should ask him by the first boon that Bharata, your son, must be proclaimed as the prince regent or the king of Ayodhya. All the arrangements made for Rama's coronation should be used for Bharata's coronation. For the second boon, ask that Rama should be exiled to a formidable forest, wearing the bark of the trees and matted locks for fourteen years. Kaikeyi, do this for Bharata's sake, for your own sake, and finally, for my sake. Trust me and do all I say for your own good. Kaikeyi, remove that *sari*. Make your hair disheveled so that it will scatter over your face and back. Open the cages and make the parrots fly away. Let the clothes and things be thrown here and there. I will go out and pluck all the plants in the garden and throw them away. While the king is entering your room, you should be rolling on the ground, writhing with pain. Everything will be all right provided you scrupulously follow my instructions." Saying thus, the hunchbacked Manthara, the repository of all evil, completely spoiled the mind of Kaikeyi. Kaikeyi hugged her ignorantly, just as a drowning man hugs a crocodile thinking that it will save him!

It was midnight. Satisfied with all the preparations going on for the coronation ceremony of Rama, King Dasharatha wanted to make his queen, Kaikeyi, very happy with this news. So he came to her palace. To his astonishment, the garden through which he used to go to the palace looked like a cremation ground. Kaikeyi, who used to meet him at the main gate with flower garlands and perfume in her hand, was not to be seen. The flowers were strewn here and there. There were no maidservants or anyone else visible. Kaikeyi was not in her room. Searching for her in different rooms, finally Dasharatha came to her wrath chamber. There he saw his queen fallen on the ground even as a celestial nymph knocked down from heaven. With her hair disheveled, clothes torn, and ornaments thrown here and there, she was crying and heaving deep sighs. Dasharatha ran to her and tried to lift her up, even as a male elephant rushes to console a female elephant struck by the sharp arrow of a hunter. Kaikeyi cried bitterly and never stopped crying. King Dasharatha, fondling her, spoke thus, "Kaikeyi, don't you know among the queens, you are the most dear to me. Did you forget that I love you because you are the most beautiful and very obedient queen? I know why you are angry at me today. But I know I can make you happy by giving you the happiest news. Listen. Rama, whom I love more than my life, Rama, who is dearer than Bharata to you, will be proclaimed as the prince-regent of our kingdom tomorrow. I should have conveyed the news to you long ago, but unfortunately, as the notice was short, I had to make vast arrangements. Come on, get up. Are you not happy with this most noble decision of mine? O Kaikeyi, someone must have pained you deeply. Why don't you tell me who caused this agony to you? Whosoever he might be, I shall see that he is properly punished. My love for you is so much that I am prepared to do whatever you want me to do. Do you want me to hang someone, even though he is innocent? Do you want me to set someone free, even though he is a miscreant? Do you want me to get the milk of a lioness? Do you want me to get anything for you from anywhere? O Kaikeyi, why don't you tell me the cause of your grief?"

Seeing Kaikeyi not responding, King Dasharatha felt very sad and to make his wife happy, he said to her, "O my queen, if you do not trust me by my words, I swear in the name of my beloved Rama that I shall fulfill any desire of yours promptly and instantaneously." Hearing these words of her husband, Queen Kaikeyi wiped her crocodile tears and sat by the king, saying, "My Lord, thank you for your kind words. You are born of the Solar race. The kings born of the Solar race never lie. You love Rama more than your life, and you have sworn in his name. I am sure you will never go back from your words. O king, I hope you remember, long ago, when you had to fight with a demon, I sat as your charioteer and saved your life twice. In order to honor me, you promised me two boons of my choice. I have treasured those boons all these years without asking you anything. Now the time has come for me to ask for those two boons from you. I am happy you have sworn in the name of your beloved Rama. O lion among the kings of the Solar race, if you go back from your promise, you will be drowned in the most heinous hell. Therefore, you better fulfill these two boons of mine.

"O king, by the first boon I want you to proclaim my son Bharata as the king of Ayodhya. Let all the preparations made for the installation of Rama be used for the installation of my son. By the second boon, I want you to exile Rama to the forest for fourteen years with the bark of trees as his clothes and matted locks as his ornament. Other than these two boons, nothing can make me happy. Without the fulfillment of your promise to me, your soul shall not reach heaven. Fulfill these two boons of mine promptly and instantaneously."

Hearing these cruel words of Kaikeyi, noble King Dasharatha fell unconscious, even as a great tree felled by the sharp hatchet of a woodcutter. For a long time, Dasharatha could not regain consciousness. After a while he gathered his senses and was repeating the name of

Rama again and again. Stung by the poisonous words of his most beloved wife, Dasharatha fell unconscious again. Then, regaining consciousness, he asked Kaikeyi, saying, "O Kaikeyi, am I dreaming? Is it doubt in my own words that haunts me or did you speak those words? I don't think you did, for you are so noble and kind. I definitely know that you love Rama more than your own son Bharata. I also know that Rama has greater respect for you than his own mother. I have never seen anyone at any time hating Rama even in their dream. Rama is loved by everybody. Rama has never pained anyone. Rama is my eldest son and deserves to be proclaimed as the king of Ayodhya. He has the right to become king. I don't understand how you can ask such boons. Are you the same Kaikeyi whom I loved before? O noble lady, perhaps you wanted to test my love for Rama. Whether you said it as a joke or seriously, please take back your words. I have consulted all the important heads of our city. I have taken advice from Brahma-rishi Vasishta and Vamadeva because I was seeing my body without my head in a dream, which has been interpreted as my approaching death. Therefore, I hurried in taking such an immediate decision to make God-like Rama take over the responsibility of the kingdom.

"Kaikeyi, my whole cabinet has agreed with me and vast arrangements have already been made. Sri Rama has already been advised by me and Sage Vasishta to fast and meditate throughout the night. All the citizens of Ayodhya are decorating the entire city and tomorrow Pushya star will be ascending and that being the auspicious moment, Rama shall be proclaimed as the prince regent of our kingdom. Kaikeyi, please, for God's sake, withdraw your words. I have lived so long. I want to die with peace. Do not try to bind me and suffocate my soul during the evening of my life. Kaikeyi, if you insist that I should fulfill your desires, then I am definitely going to die. All people of Ayodhya will curse you and

God's anger shall fall on you. Your son Bharata, who loves Rama as God, shall never agree with you, for what you speak is not *dharma*. Please save me by taking back your words."

Kaikeyi said, "O king, if you want to go to hell, I can take back my words. Now can you, who is born of Solar race, break your promise?"

Kaikeyi's words cut to the quick and the king was utterly stunned, not knowing what to do. His head began to reel and he again fell unconscious. After a while he regained consciousness and said, "Kaikeyi, I thought you were a princess of noble disposition. Now I find that you are a terrible monstress who is against *dharma*. Just like a deer is entrapped when it comes to hear the music played by the hunter, similarly, I was enchanted by your beauty and now my soul is entrapped by your senseless actions. Kaikeyi, I am worried very much by what is going to happen to my beloved Ramachandra. What will Sita think of me? The virtuous life which I have led all these years is destroyed by your selfish motives. Did Rama harm you at any time? I can imagine, out of your selfishness, you wanting to have your son proclaimed as king. But I do not understand why beloved Rama is to be exiled to the forest for fourteen years; neither do I understand why Prince Rama should wear the bark robes and matted locks and live in a forest. Your son Bharata will not like this. All sages and saints will curse you for your cruel decision. O Kaikeyi, my state is like a man lifting a deadly cobra, mistaking it to be a rope. I believed you to be bringing peace; instead you destroyed all my *dharma* and peace. This is not you, the real you. Definitely someone has poisoned your mind. I can see you are possessed by a devil and therefore you are hating Sri Rama. My state is like a man who saw the well at night and fell into it during the daytime. There is only one way through which you can save me, your soul, and make all Ayodhya happy, and that is to withdraw your words.

Kaikeyi, it is near morning and throughout the night, people have been decorating the city. Rama and Sita have been observing fast and meditation. Great sages have arrived to chant the *Vedic mantras* and to conduct the coronation ceremonies. Our royal elephant is decked and ready to take Rama in procession. *Dharma* upholds and sustains the individual and society, whereas *adharma* or unrighteousness brings peacelessness to everybody. One who protects *dharma* will be protected by *dharma*. This is a universal law. Therefore, allow Rama's coronation and give all your cooperation in doing this noble task successfully."

Hearing these words of the king, Kaikeyi was enraged. Hissing like a cobra, she bit the king with her poisonous words. "O king," she said, "are you not ashamed to take back the words of promise you have given to me long ago? What does it matter to me if all are unhappy as long as my son becomes the king? Do you mean to say that I should live like a slave of Rama's mother, Kausalya? Do you want to see my son Bharata, bereft of any position, suffer lifelong? No matter what you say, I am firm in decision. Let the preparations of Rama's coronation be used for Bharata's installation. Let Rama meditate in the forest with the sages for fourteen years."

King Dasharatha again fell on the ground crying, "Rama, Rama." Rolling with great agony, he said, "O wretched Kaikeyi, you are no longer my queen. You are a demoness. You and Bharata may have to rule over Ayodhya without the support of the people. I am going to die by separation from Rama. People of Ayodhya might leave the city and you and your son may have to live alone. O God, why has this curse come to me during the evening of my life? Where did all those effects of good and meritorious deeds which I did throughout my life go? Did I separate children from their parents in my past life or destroy the marriage of any noble couple so as to suffer this way?

"Hey Rama, you have never harmed anybody. Never at any time did you do any wrong. What right have I to banish you to the forest when you have every right to become the king of Ayodhya? How shall I show my face to you tomorrow when you and Sita will be ready, and millions of people will be waiting to receive you as their king as you are led in procession? If I hesitate crowning you and proclaiming you as the regent of our kingdom, then won't Brahma-rishi Vasishta curse me? Won't Kausalya and Sumitra be broken-hearted? O God, relieve me somehow from this agony. I am afraid of breaking the promise given to Kaikeyi long ago, and I am also afraid of fulfilling it. If I fulfill her wishes, then I will be breaking the promise which I have given to my people and Rama. O sun, do not rise. Oh darkest night, please continue forever, as you continue for cosmic dissolution. If it is morning, then I cannot show my face to Rama or my people. I think I am going to die. This is my *karma*." Saying thus, Dasharatha swooned again.

It was morning. Sages were chanting *Vedic mantras*. Rama and Sita bathed and offered their morning oblations to the sun god, chanting the *Gayatri mantra*. Decorating himself, Sri Rama, leaving Sita in her palace, mounted over Shatrunjaya elephant. Thousands and thousands of people hailed, "Victory to Rama." Sages and devotees sang, "Sri Rama Jaya Rama Jaya Jaya Rama." Protocol was observed according to the meticulous details worked out by the minister, Sumantra. The only two who were missing were King Dasharatha and Kaikeyi. Sumantra himself went to Kaikeyi's palace to find out what was happening. There he found the king lying on the ground and Kaikeyi comfortably seated on her throne. Relentlessly, Queen Kaikeyi stopped Sumantra from awakening the king and said, "O Sumantra, the king couldn't sleep throughout the night. He is resting now. If Rama is interested in seeing him, let him come here. Tell him that these are the words of his stepmother, Kaikeyi."

Sumantra left the palace quietly and came to Rama, who was seated on the royal elephant. He conveyed the words of Kaikeyi to him and Rama respectfully descended from the elephant and said to Sumantra, "If my mother Kaikeyi wants me to meet my father, out of reverence to my father I would walk the distance." Lakshmana and Sumantra accompanied Rama to Kaikeyi's palace.

No sooner Rama saw the sad plight of his father, who was writhing with pain, than he rushed to his side, saying, "My beloved father, your eldest son, Rama, is making obeisance to you. What happened to you? Please tell me if there is anything I can do." Hearing the nectarian words of his son, Dasharatha opened his tear-filled eyes, saying, "Rama, Rama." He embraced him and swooned again. Rama turned to his stepmother Kaikeyi and saluted her, saying, "O mother, may I know the cause of father's illness? May I know if there is anything I can do to make him happy?" Kaikeyi sternly replied, "Rama, you are the cause of his agony, and you can certainly help him to relieve his pain." Rama said, "Mother, I am ready to do anything if it pleases my father. Throwing myself from the mountain, plunging into the fire or river, drinking the deadliest poison are nothing for me, if it could please my father, whom I treat as God. You are my beloved mother who is also like a Goddess to me and you can tell me what is in the mind of my father. I shall carry it out without a moment's hesitation." Kaikeyi was very happy to hear these words. She said, "Rama, you are the worthy son of a worthy father. Let me tell you what is in the mind of your father. Long ago, during a battle that was fought among celestials and demons, your father was invited to help the celestials. I was assisting your father as I was his beloved queen. During the battle, I saved him twice. Pleased with this, he promised me two boons which I treasured since that time. Last night I asked him to fulfill those two boons. He swore in your name that he would fulfill whatever I asked. For my first boon, I asked him to install Bharata instead of you as the prince regent of Ayodhya. For my second boon, I asked him to send you to the forest adorned with bark robes and matted locks to perform austerities for fourteen years. Your father wants to fulfill his promise but he is afraid to carry it out due to his attachment for you. Now you can relieve him by carrying out his promises to me. You alone can make your father happy by telling of your preparedness to fulfill his words of promise to me. If you do not, then your father will die with great agony and that sin will sit on your head."

Sri Rama was neither depressed nor troubled at heart by hearing these words of Kaikeyi. Instead, he was very happy. He said, "Mother, I am privileged to serve my father and go to the forest to fulfill his words of promise to you. Bharata is very dear to me and I am delighted that he will be the king of Ayodhya. What could be a greater blessing than to go to the forest to meditate with the sages? I declare, O mother, that I will fulfill father's promise to you. This is the simplest thing for me to do. I would have done it long ago if father would have informed me. Let Bharata be king and I shall go to the forest for fourteen years with the bark of trees as my robes and a single tress as my diadem. Please comfort my father through your service."

Kaikeyi was delighted to hear these words of Rama and asked him to start for the forest without any delay. King Dasharatha, hearing these words of Kaikeyi, became very angry. "O wretched Kaikeyi, how shall I live without Rama? Oh, Rama, Rama, Rama." Saying thus, again he fell unconscious. Sri Rama consoled him and paid his obeisance, saluted the feet of Kaikeyi and made his way to mother Kausalya's palace, accompanied by Lakshmana. Queen Kausalya, offering her prayers to the Almighty Lord, was distributing gifts munificently to the priest and the poor. She had already ordered the worship service to be conducted in all the temples of the city, in order to receive the blessings of God for an undisturbed coronation ceremony of her son. When Rama entered her palace, Kausalya ran to him with maternal affection and Rama fell at her feet with prostrated obeisance. Kausalya blessed him, saying, "My son Rama, the time for your coronation is fast approaching; I want to see the sages blessing you with red rice sprinkled over your head. As your father places the crown over your head, I want to see the gods showering flowers over you. May you shine as the illustrious king of the Solar race." Sri Rama felt very bad as he was going to make his mother sad by the news of his departure to the forest. He said, "O my beloved mother, things have changed for good and Divine Will alone pervades over our will. I have been longing to visit the mountains and forests to meditate with the *rishis.* I am thankful to my father for fulfilling this desire of mine. I have come here to receive your blessings before I enter the Dandaka forest to practice asceticism for fourteen years. My brother Bharata will be installed on the throne of Ayodhya. Such is the sweet will of my father. His wishes were conveyed to me by stepmother Kaikeyi. Please bless me so that I may fulfill the words of promise given by my father to my stepmother."

It was too much for Kausalya to take these words to her heart. At once she fell on the ground even as a plantain tree overturned by a tornado. Rama lifted her up and tried to console her by saying, "Mother, please accept the will of God. I shall return to Ayodhya very soon by spending fourteen years like fourteen hours with your blessing." Kausalya stopped and profusely shedding tears of grief, said, "O my son Rama, it would have been better if I had remained barren. Unfortunately, you took birth in my womb. Due to my ill luck, you were made to suffer. If you were born as the son of Kaikeyi, you would not have had this trouble. O Rama, my whole life is a life of grief. Since the time of marriage, I was always ill-treated by your father. After his marriage with Kaikeyi, he visited me very rarely and thus I was left with loneliness. I found light and peace only when you were born by God's blessings. It was the essence of Vishnu which was given by an angel at the conclusion of a fire-sacrifice conducted by your childless father, which bore all three queens the four children. Thus, I know that you are not a mere son but are God. Now my *karma* again makes me suffer by your separation. I don't understand anything. My heart must be made of rock not to have broken to pieces on hearing of your departure to the forest. In this life I have not done any bad deed consciously, but I might have done a great wrong in my past life; otherwise, I would not have suffered this agony. Rama, you have done no wrong to anybody. Why should Kaikeyi or your father exile you to the forest? O my dear child, I certainly cannot bear it. Kaikeyi has always insulted me and now she wants to become the queen mother and ill-treat me. I do not want to live this painful life.

"Rama, you know the *Vedas* and *Upanishads*. You want to fulfill the words of promise given by your father to your stepmother. Rama, what about me? Am I not your mother? Is not mother the first one to be worshipped as goddess and next the father? If so, as your mother, I want to tell you that you should not go to the forest. If you can fulfill the words of your father, then how can you transgress the words of your mother?"

Sri Rama said, "O my divine mother, I understand the depth of your love for me. I agree with you that I must honor your words more than that of my father. But the problem is, who is the most respected person to a wife? It is her husband. Dasharatha is your husband and for you he is God. If I should not follow his words, then it is sinful on your part to transgress the words of your husband. Therefore, O mother, making your husband peaceful seems to be the wisest way. Bless me so that I may fulfill his words."

Kausalya cried bitterly and said, "My son, I cannot

argue with you, for you know the *Vedas* better than I. All that I request is you allow me to go with you to the forest, even as the mother cow goes with her calf." Wiping her tears away, Sri Rama said, "Divine mother, my father is suffering agony at my separation. He is already very much disturbed by Kaikeyi's attitude. As a chaste wife, it behooves you to serve him at this critical hour. If you come to the forest with me, then you will not be discharging the duties of a noble wife to her husband."

Embracing her son again and again, Kausalya bathed him with her tears. Knowing that Rama was of firm decision, Kausalya spoke to Lakshmana, saying, "O Lakshmana, how shall I bear the separation of my God-like son, Rama? Why should your father, to make one woman happy, make the whole country unhappy? Is there no one in the country who can stand for the truth? Oh, why don't I die instead of living this wretched life? My heart is certainly made of stone or iron that I am still living."

Lakshmana could no more bear Kausalya's sad plight. He flew into a rage and spoke."Rama, how can King Dasharatha, who has promised the entire nation of your coronation, break his promise for the sake of fulfilling his words to Kaikeyi? How can anyone take away your right as an heir to the throne, being the eldest son of the family? Since he has decided willfully to carry out the behests of his evil queen, as a henpecked husband, I must punish him with the pain of death. I shall slay him regardless of the fact that he is my father. I shall slay all those who want to stand by him and try to deprive you of your right to the throne. I see no sin in it for they have taken to a wrong path. I shall see that you are installed on the throne."

Even as a rider controls an elephant with his goad, similarly, Sri Rama controlled Lakshmana's anger with his wisdom. He said, "Lakshmana, I know it is your love for me which makes you speak these words. But what you speak is not *dharma*. Father is like God. His words are *Vedas* for us. Is it not selfishness to kill him or harm him for the sake of this throne? As his son, how can you even think of these evil thoughts? It is not the throne, nor riches, nor even the rulership of the three worlds that is important to me; only *dharma*.

"Lakshmana, our father definitely had no intention to send me to the forest. His decision was to install me on the throne. That which has now happened is something beyond his power to change. Therefore, we have no right to blame him. Neither is it wise for us to blame our mother, Kaikeyi. She was very kind and very good to us all these years. I don't think she intended for Bharata to be coronated nor me to be exiled. For her to act like this there should be some other force, without which she would not even have dreamt about these things. In short, I call this Divine Will. There is nothing that you, or I, or anyone for that matter, can do. We only have to obey the Divine Will.

"Our father Dasharatha is a follower of *dharma*. He is afraid of what is going to happen to his soul if he breaks his words of promise given to Kaikeyi long before his decision to install me. The duty of a son is to make the father peaceful. Therefore, it is wise for me to go to the forest. Lakshmana, if we use any force, we will be acting against Divine Will and thereby we will inflict untold misery on ourselves and everyone, all because of our selfishness. Instead, if I go to the forest, I will be happy, our mother Kaikeyi will be happy and father's soul will feel peaceful at the fulfillment of his word. So be calm."

Lakshmana said, "Sri Rama, I honor you not only as my elder brother but also as God. For me you are everything. It is *dharma* for you to be the regent of Ayodhya, being the eldest son of the family. Sage Vasishta and the whole kingdom know this to be *dharma*. I don't believe in faith, destiny, or Divine Will, regarding this matter. A man of courage defeats fate and shapes his destiny as he wants. Divine Will just cooperates with such a man. It is only the weaklings who are afraid of fate and such fatalists never accomplish any success in their lives. With your grace, Sri Rama, I can prove this to everybody. The bow and the powerful arrows which I have are not just for decoration. I shall see that you are installed and be they angels, human beings, or any number of people and angels put together, I can punish them single-handedly. All I need is your grace and permission."

Sri Rama said, "Lakshmana, don't I have as much prowess as you have? Is it difficult for me to dismiss the decision of our father and install myself on the throne? Do I need anybody's help to accomplish this? Don't you know the purpose of our incarnation here? It is for the restoration of *dharma* and not to rule over a petty kingdom. The very fact that you cannot do anything without my permission and I cannot give you permission to do the unrighteous act, shows how powerful is Divine Will. Lakshmana, you know that I am not a fatalist. But in this context, I want to show that true enjoyment lies not in possessing anything but in renunciation; not in bodily pleasures, but in the peace of the spirit. Therefore, do not be angry." Saying thus, Rama wiped the tears of his beloved brother, Lakshmana. Lakshmana said, "Rama, to me you are divine. Your will be done. But please allow me to serve you forever."

Rama sought the blessings of his mother Kausalya for a successful return from the forest life. Bathing Rama with her tears, Kausalya said the following benedictional prayer. "Rama, may the earth and forest be peaceful to you. May all the gods bless you. May all the merits of my good deeds protect you. May you enjoy the company of the sages and may your meditation bring illumination to you. May the rocks and trees, pools and birds, protect you. May semigods and demigods, wind god and fire god, be propitious. May the eight guardian deities of eight directions constantly guard and protect you. May Shiva, Ganesha, Skanda, presiding deities over sun, moon, and all the planets, be your defenders at all times. Let there be no disturbance of thunder and lightning, earthquake and tornadoes on your way. O my dear son, my soul will be waiting for your return. Bring a great name to the Solar race by the protection of *dharma*. May the Holy Trinity protect you always." Having spoken thus, Queen Kausalya embraced her son Rama and kissed him on his forehead. Receiving her blessings, Rama returned to his palace accompanied by Lakshmana.

While Sita was rejoicing, thinking of the coronation of Sri Rama, Rama came with Lakshmana. Sita saw no joy on Rama's face and she asked him, "My beloved Lord, how is it that I do not see the white umbrella spread over your head? How is it that I do not see sages and saints following you, chanting the *mantras* as a part of the coronation ceremony? The auspicious hour is almost here. And how is it that you are not in a hurry to go the main palace? Pray, tell me."

Sri Rama said, "Beloved Sita, the auspicious time has now come for me to go to the forest. My brother, Bharata, will be coronated instead of me. Such is the sweet will of God and my father, King Dasharatha. This is due to the word of promise given by my father to my stepmother, Kaikeyi. My heart was aspiring to be with the sages in the forest retreats of Dandaka. It all worked out beautifully. As you know, Bharata is very dear to me and he respects you as much as he respects his own mother, Kaikeyi. As my father and my mother, Kausalya, are in great agony at my separation, it is but proper for you to be here with them to serve your father-in-law and mother-in-law. I may have to spend the forest life for just fourteen years and then I will be back to see you. So, hold your peace and be happy."

Hearing these words of her Lord, Sita burst into tears. She could not believe such words could come out of the mouth of her perfect husband. Her full moon-like face was eclipsed by the feeling of separation from Rama. It was very hard for her to believe that such changes could happen so fast. She fell on the shoulders of Rama and bathed him with her tears of grief. Then she was a bit angry and said, "Hey Rama, are you not ashamed to leave me alone here in the palace and go alone to the forest? Is it worthy of you to do that? Is it written in any scripture, Rama, that while the husband is wandering in the forest with difficulty, the wife should enjoy the palace? Can you show me such a statement in any holy scripture which you have read? Do you think I am an ignorant woman who knows not the path of virtue? I do not worry if Bharata should rule over the country. I am not worried that you should leave the kingdom and be exiled to the forest, but I am really worried about your decision to leave me alone here and go to the forest yourself. Rama, no matter what you say, I am coming with you wherever you go."

Consoling her, Sri Rama said, "Sita, I know that you know *dharma*, but you should know that my stepmother Kaikeyi, or my father the king never asked me to take you with me. Therefore, there is no point in your going with me." Hearing these words of Rama, Sita was very upset. "Rama, what is the meaning of marriage? Did Kaikeyi or your father want you to go half to the forest or full? How could a husband be full without his wife? You are half; I am your better half. If both of us go to the forest, only then will you fulfill the promise of your father to your stepmother."

"But Sita," Rama interrupted, "don't you know that the forest is not a palace? Do you know the difficulties of dwelling in a forest? There will not be timely food or rest. The path of the forest is filled with pointed stones, thorns, and as you walk you will never know which cruel animal may rush toward you or which tree may fall over you. Sita, you may have to bathe in lakes and rivers where crocodiles may make a meal of you. I haven't yet told you about the demons, ghosts, and evil spirits that dwell in the forest and may haunt us. Sita, even here in the palace I see that you easily get tired by moving from one palace to another and you need hundreds of maidservants to take care of you. There will be no one in the forest to attend you. I am not going to the forest to make a home and dwell there with my wife. I go there to be alone with sages and practice asceticism. Sita, if you are there my mind will be anxious about you, and therefore, I cannot successfully meditate. Do you understand?"

Sita flew into a fury and lashed Rama with the following words: "O cruel Rama, when I married you I thought you were a man. Now I see you look like a man and act like a woman. Rama, you are a real poet. You describe the forest and animals so beautifully. Did you forget to tell about mountains and their dangers, monkeys, and cobras? Rama, why are you carrying that Kodanda bow and the inexhaustible arrow? Is it for decoration? Enough of these lame excuses. I know who you are. Before I married you I saw with my own eyes your prowess when you snapped the Shiva bow into two. I have also heard the stories of your destroying the demons Tataka and Subahu and how you vanquished demon Mareecha by making him fly across the seven seas with your sharp arrow. Do not try to fool me. Rama, wherever you are there is no fear of ghosts, demons, or evil spirits. Nor is there any fear of any cruel animals or serpents. Rama, I know that you are God. I cannot stay without you even for a millionth fraction of a moment. Wherever you dwell, that is heaven for me. The forest where you dwell is Ayodhya for me and Ayodhya without you is a veritable hell for me. Rama, I promise you. Please listen. I shall never ask for anything but I shall go ahead of you in the forest to remove the sharp stones and thorns and make your way smooth. I shall pluck the delicious fruits and feed you. I shall pluck the leaves of the trees and spread them over the grass to make a soft bed for you. I shall knead your feet, gaze at your beauty, and feast my eyes. I will be of immense help to you because I come there to serve you rather than to be served. Please, please Rama, do not leave me here. Take me with you."

Seeing his wife crying bitterly, Rama's heart melted, but restraining his feelings, the lion among men spoke to that embodiment of virtue, thus, "Sita, I don't know what is going to happen if I take you with me. I am also worried who will take care of your father-in-law and mother-in-law here. I have stopped my mother from coming with me, asking her to be with her husband to serve him. For that is the foremost duty of a wife." Taking that as an opportunity, Sita said, "Rama, that is the wonderful truth. A wife should be with her husband serving him. If this is what you said to your mother that she should be with your father to serve him, doesn't the same law apply in my case? Is it not *dharma* for me to go with my husband and serve him? Rama, when I married you, my father Janaka taught me that I should follow you like a shadow. One very important point I want to bring to your attention, Rama. Before I married you, while I was living at my father's palace, a sagely astrologer told me that I have forest dwelling *karma* for a few years. Rama, this is true. Suppose you do not take me with you, then according to my *karma* I may have to dwell in another forest. Would you like that? Or, I can suffer that *karma* with great joy if I go with you. What do you say?"

Immediately Rama said, "Sita, all right then. Come with me but be prepared for the inevitable difficulties."

Then Lakshmana fell at the feet of Rama and Sita and said, "O my divine parents, please do not leave your son here. Even though Dasharatha and Sumitra are my physical parents, you are my divine parents. I depend on you, love you as God and Goddess, and serve you with my thought, word, and deed. This I consider as the foremost duty of my life."

Rama said, "Lakshmana, I know you love me and you have been with me always from childhood. I know it is very difficult for me to live without you, but Lakshmana, don't you realize that you are married to Urmila, who needs your attention?"

Lakshmana said, "Urmila constantly meditates on you both. She is ready to offer me to serve you. This I have discussed with her long ago. She knows that my life is dedicated to your service. Please take me with you."

Sri Rama could not deny the prayerful request of his beloved brother, Lakshmana. He gave his permission for Lakshmana to go with him to the forest.

Now Rama, Lakshmana, and Sita began distributing all their wealth to the poor and the needy. Hundreds and thousands of people were blessed by the munificent gifts given by them. It so happened, there was a priest who was very poor. He thought of becoming very rich by the gifts which Rama was distributing. He saw thousands of well-fed cows yielding rich milk, whose horns were decorated with gold. He requested Rama to give him as many cows as he could cover by throwing his stick from the place where Rama was standing. The benevolent Lord Rama wanted to please the poor *brahmin* and allowed him to do so. He was so thin and weak that people thought he may not cover the space occupied by even one hundred cows but to their astonishment, when the priest threw the stick with all his might, it covered the space of all the thousands of cows standing there. Rama smiled and said, "Even though the body of the priest is weak, his desire is very strong." Saying thus, Rama gave all those cows, whose horns were decorated with gold, to that poor priest who became rich.

After the distribution of all their wealth, Rama, Sita,

and Lakshmana came to the palace of Kaikeyi. Saluting King Dasharatha, Rama said, "O my beloved father, I am ready to go to the forest to fulfill your words of promise to Kaikeyi. Along with me, Sita and Lakshmana are also coming. However I tried, I could not stop them from coming." Dasharatha groaned. "Rama, please take me as well. I cannot live without you, even as the body cannot live without the soul." Rama said, "Father, you should be here to see Kaikeyi's son Bharata installed. Without any delay, please send swift messengers to bring Bharata to the palace and make Kaikeyi and all citizens of Ayodhya very happy by proclaiming him to be the regent of Ayodhya. Please give Bharata my love and blessings."

Dasharatha requested Rama to stay at least that night with him and start the next morning. Rama said that good things should not be postponed and he must go to the forest immediately, without further delay, so that his words of promise to Kaikeyi are fulfilled. Thereby, King Dasharatha ordered Sumantra to prepare everything needed to make the forest dwelling of Rama a joyful one. He said, "O Sumantra, fill many chariots full of gold and wealth, grains and vegetables, milk and honey, for their happy forest dwelling." Kaikeyi heard these words and was much agonized. She said, "Do you want to leave the kingdom like a desert to be ruled by my son, Bharata? Is this the fulfillment of the words of your promise? As per my boon which you have given to me, Rama should go to the forest only with matted locks and bark garments."

Rama said, "Oh my beloved father, what my mother Kaikeyi says is true. Would anyone like to carry the chains after the elephant has been given away? When I am not interested in the kingdom of Ayodhya, am I interested in these things to be carried from here to the forest? We are not going to the forest to enjoy our life there as if we dwell in the city. All that we need is a blessing." Turning toward Kaikeyi, Rama said, "Mother, I am ready to wear the bark of trees." Kaikeyi, who had kept them ready, brought the bark of the trees and gave it to Sri Rama. Then and there, Rama threw away all his ornaments and wore the bark garments and the matted locks. Seeing this, Dasharatha cried with agony, "O sinful Kaikeyi, your soul shall never find peace for bringing this pain to everyone." Meanwhile, Kaikeyi brought the bark robes to Lakshmana and Sita as well. Lakshmana wore them, but Sita, who was not accustomed to wearing the bark of trees, came to Rama and with all innocence, asked him how to wear it. When Sri Rama wrapped the bark of the trees around her body, all those who were present sighed deeply. Until that time, Brahma-rishi Vasishta was holding his anger. Seeing Sita chastised in such an insulting way, he spoke to Kaikeyi angrily. "Shame on you, O Queen Kaikeyi. Whichever good or bad *karma* a man does, he will enjoy or suffer the consequences, inevitably. Kaikeyi, there is no end to your sinful deeds. Out of your selfishness you pained your righteous husband, exiled God-like Rama to the forest, and brought pain and shame to the entire Solar race. A whole generation will curse you for the wrongs you have done. No one would like to stay in Ayodhya under your rule." Hearing the words of Vasishta, thousands of people joined with him, saying, "We don't want to stay in Ayodhya under the rule of Kaikeyi! We will renounce everything and go with Sri Rama and dwell in the forest." Before Dasharatha could once again embrace him, Rama, of firm resolve, sat in the chariot of Sumantra, along with Sita and Lakshmana, and left for the forest.

Sumantra was deputed by the king to take them to the bank of the Ganges and return. The horses of his chariot cried bitterly that they could not carry Rama to the forest. The flag of his chariot fluttered, which proved the denial of Rama's exile by the entire city of Ayodhya. Hundreds and thousands of men, women, and aged couples ran behind the chariot renouncing their hearth and home. Blessing everybody from the chariot, Rama maintained equanimity. Thousands of people stood on their terraces and balconies bathed in tears, as if their joy had gone. All animals and birds of Ayodhya fasted. Other than Kaikeyi and Manthara, no one was happy.

Ayodhya, without Rama, looked like a desert. Thinking this to be the greatest curse to the Solar race, the sun set. Pitch darkness encompassed everybody in Ayodhya, both within and without. Evil ghosts and astral spirits filled the air. Ayodhya, which had looked like the Kingdom of Heaven, was converted into a dark hell by the disappearance of Sri Rama, Sita, and Lakshmana. A bemoaning cry issued forth from every palace with the Holy Name, "Rama, Rama." King Dasharatha sank in the ocean of sorrow, never to come up again. Queen Kausalya and Sumitra sat around his body with a grief that was beyond description. Kaikeyi rejoiced with her maid-servant, the hunchbacked, cruel Manthara!

Sri Rama's chariot reached the bank of Tamasa river. As it was night, Rama decided to rest there at the foot of a tree. Lakshmana arranged the soft, natural bed of leaves and grass for Rama and Sita. Hundreds and thousands of people who had been running behind the chariot of Rama slept soundly due to their great fatigue. Sri Rama could not sleep, feeling pity for everybody. He arose at midnight, called Sumantra and said, "O noble minister, you have been very kind in carrying out the orders of my father in bringing us here. Your duty ends by taking us to the bank of the river Ganges. Please take us right now, as everyone is sleeping. If we wait until morning, then all these thousands of people will follow me to the forest and suffer there unnecessarily. I do not want to inflict misery on anyone, nor cause peacelessness in the calm forest retreats of the sages by taking thousands of people from the city. It is good for them to go back to Ayodhya and perform their duties and live there. I know how they will feel but in the interests of the future work that is given to me, I have to follow my conscience. Pray

Sumantra, take Sita, Lakshmana, and me to the bank of the Ganges without any delay."

Immediately, the obedient Sumantra brought his chariot and took all of them away from those people who were resting, without anyone knowing they were leaving. After a few hours, they reached the bank of the river Ganges. When the people awoke, they couldn't see Rama, Sita, or Lakshmana and they blamed Minister Sumantra for taking their Rama away from them. Cursing their own fate, they returned to Ayodhya with great agony, pacifying themselves with the hope that if they followed *dharma*, Rama would give them *darshan*, at least after fourteen years.

The village near the Ganges is named Shringiberapura. It was ruled by a boatman named Guha. He was very devoted to Sri Rama, but until then he had never had the *darshan* of the Lord. He gathered hundreds of his people around Rama and prayed Rama to stay in his village. Knowing that Rama was exiled to the forest, Guha said, "Sri Rama, our village is beyond the jurisdiction of Kaikeyi and Bharata. You can spend your fourteen years very happily here and we, your devotees, will serve you, Lakshmana, and Mother Sita. Pray, Rama, our God, stay with us."

Rama said, "Beloved Guha, I am very grateful for your prayerful request but I must go, as per my duty. Please prepare your boat and take us across the Ganges without any delay, lest the people of Ayodhya come in large numbers." Guha allowed Sita and Lakshmana to sit in his boat. When Rama was about to enter the boat, Guha stopped him, saying, "Rama, I am sorry. I cannot allow you to touch my boat with the dust of your feet." Rama asked him to explain. Guha said, "Sri Rama, I have heard enough stories about the power of the dust of your holy feet. I have heard how a rock was transformed into a woman named Ahalya when the pollen of your feet fell on the rock in which she was entrapped. I want to tell you, Rama, that my boat is made of wood. If a rock was transformed into a woman, I have every right to fear that my wooden boat would be transformed into a woman also. Rama, this boat is the only means of subsistence for my family. Until you allow me to wash your feet to take away the dust, so long I will not allow you to enter into the boat." Sri Rama saw his noble intention of worshipping his feet and he allowed him to do so. With great devotion, Guha worshipped the feet of Rama, carried Sri Rama on his shoulders, and danced with his people, chanting, "Sitaram, Sitaram." Blessing all his people, Rama entered his boat.

Rama saw Sumantra and the horses shedding tears profusely at the separation from the Lord. "Take me with you, Rama," cried Sumantra. "How shall I go back to the deserted Ayodhya? What shall I tell your beloved father?" Rama said, "Sumantra, each has a duty toward me in his life. Your duty was to bring me to the Ganges and then go back with my blessings. Please realize that I love you and I want you to tell my father that I shall carry out his order. Please convey my salutations to all the mothers, especially Kaikeyi, who gave me this privilege of serving *dharma*." Sita sent her love to all as Lakshmana was silently watching from the boat.

As Sumantra returned toward Ayodhya, Guha took the divine couple and Lakshmana across the Ganges. Sri Rama thanked Guha and inquired of his charges. Guha said, "Rama, by your grace I have taken you across the river Ganges. You kindly take me across the ocean of rebirth." Rama blessed Guha by embracing him and blessing him with *bhakti*, or pure love. Guha also wanted to follow Rama to the forest but Rama stopped him, saying, "Guha, just like Sumantra had a duty of bringing us from Ayodhya up to the bank of the Ganges, similarly, your duty ended by taking us across the Ganges." In the scheme of an *avatar*, each has been given a duty to fulfill. By the performance of that duty, they attain God's grace.

When Guha returned, as per the will of Rama, Sita performed a worship to Mother Ganges. Offering flowers into the waters of the Ganges, Sita prayed with joined palms. "O Mother Ganges, you have sprung from the toe of Vishnu and flowed from the matted locks of Shiva. Please bless us to complete our task in our forest life and return successfully. I shall once again offer my *puja* to you on returning. Salutations." Saying thus, Sita and Rama, along with Lakshmana, began their journey for the forest life.

They reached the holy hermitage of Sage Bharadvaja. The holy sage received them with great devotion and offered them fruits and shelter. Bharadvaja, along with his disciples, sang the glory of Rama and said that his austerities were fruitful by the *darshan* of Rama and Sita. He requested Rama to spend the period of his exile in his *ashram*. Sri Rama told the sage to show him a noble spot in the mountains where he could stay with Sita and Lakshmana. Sage Bharadvaja gave him directions to a beautiful mountain named Chitrakuta. The sage said, "Many sages and ascetics meditate on that mountain, having their small hermitages. Give them your *darshan* and protect them from the demons."

Thereafter, Rama, Sita, and Lakshmana took leave of Sage Bharadvaja and his disciples. They crossed the holy Yamuna river and Sita worshipped that holy river also. They meditated under a holy tree called Nyagrodha and offered their worship there. For them the entire nature was the expression of God. Enjoying the beauty of the forest, they had a smooth journey. Rama was moving ahead, followed by Sita, and Lakshmana was protecting Sita by following her. Saint Tulasidas describes: "In between Rama and Lakshmana, Sita was shining, like *maya* between God and soul." The Saint explains the truth of *Vedanta* with this illustration. Lakshmana is compared to the soul, Rama to God, and Sita is *maya*—the power of God that veils the soul. It is only by surrendering to this Universal Mother one reaches God.

On their way to Chitrakuta mountain, Sri Rama would describe to Sita the panoramic beauty of nature to keep her happy. "O my dear Sita, look at the tall trees that kiss the clouds. Look at those beautiful birds of colored wings singing different melodies. It seems the cruel animals have given up their ferocity and they act in amity with one another. Don't you see a lion there with its mane coiled around the horn of a deer and a fox is disentangling the lion's mane from the horn of that deer? It is unusual to see such friendship between the lion and the deer. There, near that tree, O Sita, a mongoose and a cobra are playing together. This should definitely be a holy place where the *rishis* dwell and meditate. The high spiritual vibration of this place feels very soothing and somewhere near here should be Chitrakuta mountain. Even though we miss all our people of Ayodhya, still we feel so happy and peaceful in this forest." Speaking thus, Rama soothed the journey and they arrived at Chitrakuta.

Lakshmana built a beautiful hut for their dwelling. He especially designed a private room for Sita and Rama in that hut. When Rama saw this, he embraced Lakshmana and said, "O brother Lakshmana, you are really not only my brother but also my father. Like a father who takes care of the comforts of his married son, you have so kindly built this special room for Sita and me." Lakshmana politely said, "Sri Rama, all that I care is to remain as your servant. Bless me to serve you and Sita." The three of them dwelt in the hermitage happily.

Sumantra returned to Ayodhya and conveyed the tidings sent by Rama and Sita to King Dasharatha. Again and again, Dasharatha, Kausalya, Sumitra, and others, inquired of Sumantra about Rama, Lakshmana, and Sita. Sumantra explained everything to them and tried to console them as much as he could. King Dasharatha was very weak, lamenting over all that had happened and cursing his own fate. That night, Kausalya, who was by his side, heard him narrating an old story.

"O Queen Kausalya," sobbed the king, "I know now why all these things have happened. Long before I married you, I was very much interested in hunting. I was a great archer who could hit an animal by mere sound. Being proud of my ability in archery, one night I was sitting on the branch of a huge tree ready to kill the cruel animals. From a great distance I heard some animal drinking water from a river. Taking that to be the sound of an animal, I hit the arrow toward that direction and I heard an ascetic crying with agony, 'Oh, I am dying.' I was afraid that I did a wrong deed and I rushed to the spot. There I saw a great ascetic rolling on the ground, bathing in his blood. I fell at his feet and prayed for forgiveness. The ascetic said, 'O noble king, I have forgiven you, but I am worried about my aged, blind parents whom I left a few steps distance from here. Sage Shravana and his wife are my aged parents. My name is Shraavana, being the son of Shravana. O king, as according to the tradition, my parents have only one desire in their old age and that is to go to Kashi, Benares, and leave their bodies there. To fulfill that desire, I was serving them and carrying them on my shoulders. On my way to Kashi, I came to this forest and my parents were very thirsty. For this reason I came here to fetch water. It is my ill luck which has brought my end here. Could you carry my body to my parents and tell them what has happened? Please perform my obsequies and then carry my aged parents to Kashi and leave them there. They want to meditate there until the end of their lives. If you could do this much of a favor for me, I part with this body peacefully.'

"O Kausalya, saying thus, that great ascetic took his breath to the brow center and departed from the body chanting the holy *Om* syllable. Thereafter, I carried his body to his parents. Hearing my footsteps, the old parents thought their son was coming. Lovingly they said, 'Beloved son Shraavana, you took such great pains in bringing water to us. Your delay caused us apprehension. Come our son, we would like to embrace you and bless you.' Kausalya, I was speechless. My throat was parched and my body trembled before that blind, sagely couple. I kept the body of their son near them and offered the water to them, saying, 'O divine, sagely couple, I am not your son. I am Dasharatha, the prince of Ayodhya. I came for hunting and unfortunately, mistaking your son for an animal, I hit him by my arrow. Hearing his cry, I went near him and he told me to tell you everything and he peacefully left his body, giving me an opportunity to serve you by taking you to the holy pilgrimage center, Kashi. Please accept this water and forgive me for the greatest sin I have committed without knowing.'

"O Kausalya," the king continued "hearing the sad demise of their son by my arrow, Sage Shravana's wife died instantaneously out of great sorrow. Sage Shravana embraced the dead body of his son and lamented over his loss. Despite his knowledge of truth, he bathed his son's body with tears of affection and glorified him. Thereafter, turning to me, the great sage uttered a curse. 'O Dasharatha, arrogantly you killed my innocent son who was pure and noble. You have taken away the sight of my eyes and the light of my life by killing him. I cannot touch the water which you have brought, O sinful wretch. However I try, I cannot forgive you, for you may have to suffer your *karma*. Even as I die by the separation from my son, similarly, let your death take place by the separation from your son; no one can change this destiny of yours.' Cursing thus, Kausalya, that great sage died there instantaneously. Today I remember those words of that great sage which I had totally forgotten all these years. *Karma* has a long hand to reach a man who has done the *karma*, wherever he goes."

As the king was narrating his story, he found

everyone around him, including Kausalya, had gone to sleep due to great fatigue. There was no one to hear his sad story nor to pour a drop of Ganges water into his mouth at the time of his death. Crying with great agony and remembering the name of Rama, that great King Dasharatha died. The next morning Kausalya and Sumitra found the king was dead. The entire kingdom mourned. Sage Vasishta consulted Sage Markandeya and sent a few messengers to convey this sad message to Bharata and Shatrughna and bring them back to Ayodhya. Meanwhile, the body of the king was kept in a vat of oil until Bharata's arrival. All people blamed Kaikeyi whose selfishness brought misery to everyone.

The very night when the messengers reached the city, Bharata had a bad dream and he narrated the contents of the dream to Shatrughna and others the next morning. He said, "I saw my father in this dream, his hair scattered, falling from a mountain into a pit. He was drinking oil and he was weeping at times and laughing at times. Later I saw him eating some rice mixed with sesame seed. The bad dream continued and I saw an earthquake and stars and the moon falling on the earth. Then I saw my father donned with black cloth, decked with red flower garlands, traveling in a southern direction, seated in a chariot drawn by donkeys. I saw a demoness taking the king away. For me, this was not a mere dream. I think my father is ill or something bad is going to happen or has already happened. I want to go to Ayodhya and until I see my father and Sri Rama, my soul will not be peaceful."

As Bharata was talking to his people about the dream, the messengers from Ayodhya arrived. They never conveyed any bad news to him but only requested him to return to Ayodhya with Shatrughna without any delay. Bharata's maternal uncle and his grandfather gave him costly gifts. Receiving their blessings, Bharata and Shatrughna, traveling day and night in their chariots drawn by swiftly moving horses, reached Ayodhya in approximately seven days. They saw the city looking like a desert. Plants and trees of the garden had almost died. A few people who were moving on the road cursed Bharata no sooner they saw him. Shops were all closed and the whole city looked like a cremation ground. Speaking to Shatrughna of his apprehensions, he went directly to the palace of his mother, Kaikeyi, and ran to her chamber with Shatrughna as quickly as he could. No sooner he saw his mother he saluted her according to the tradition and asked her, saying, "O mother, how is my beloved father? Where is my God Rama whom I worship like a father? Where is my beloved Lakshmana? How is Sita, whom I worship as Goddess? Why is it that the city of Ayodhya looks to my eyes as a desert or a cremation ground? Why am I not seeing the round, red mark on your forehead, the sacred symbol of a married woman according to our tradition. Please tell me everything."

Kaikeyi smiled and said, "My dear son, I have done all that is possible for me to make you happy. I have done something great to make your position unshakeable. Do not worry about your father or Rama or Sita. By the timely advice of dear Manthara, I have seen that all good should come to you. Your father, due to his old age and worry, has passed away and is happy in heaven." No sooner Bharata heard these words, his head reeled and he swooned. Shatrughna also fell unconscious for some time. Both of them gathered their senses after a while. Now Bharata asked his mother the cause of the death of his father and also the whereabouts of Sri Rama. Kaikeyi said, "My beloved son, your father organized the coronation of Rama with wrong intention, to deceive you and me. He never sent word to you nor told me earlier but secretly arranged everything for the installation of Rama as the king of Ayodhya. Fortunately, destiny was on our side so Manthara inspired me to do that which is right. Long ago your father gave me two boons that I treasured all these years. I made him swear in the name of Rama to fulfill his boons and he agreed. By the first boon I asked him to install you as the king of Ayodhya with the same preparations made for Rama's coronation. By the second boon I asked him to exile Rama to the formidable forest for fourteen long years. Having his plans shattered, your father sank in the ocean of sorrow. He could neither break his word to me nor install Rama. Rama went to the forest with Sita and Lakshmana, with matted locks and bark garments, which I readily supplied. Your father died due to the pain of separation from Rama. Now my son, your way is clear. The whole kingdom is yours. The throne of Ayodhya is waiting for you; I will be glad to install you as the king of Ayodhya."

Hearing these words of Kaikeyi, Bharata flew into a rage and he drew his sharp-edged sword to kill his mother. Knitting his brow and biting his lips, hissing with indignation, Bharata was about to knock his mother down and sever her head from the trunk. Sage Vasishta stopped him from any wrongdoing. With mixed feelings of anger, grief, and separation from Rama and Sita, Bharata reproached his mother, saying, "O cruel lady, you are unworthy to be called mother by me. You are a cruel demoness who has brought great shame to our Solar race. Never before has anyone done such harm to the race and society as you have done with your selfishness. I have never seen you at any time having any unkindness toward anybody. You loved Rama more than me. You respected my father as God. What devil possessed you? How could you think of sending Sri Rama to the forest? What wrong has he done to you, me, or anyone else? Due to his exile, our kind father also passed away, suffering. People will think that I am the source of all this evil. Truly speaking, I am innocent of all these things. The curse of my father is on my head. I do not know what Rama and Lakshmana are thinking about me. Could there be any greater sin than sending that Divine Mother Sita with bark garments to the forest? O my God, O Rama, what shall I do? Where shall I go? To whom shall I tell my agony? How could the earth hold such cruel people like you, O Kaikeyi? Why doesn't the sky fall on my head or death snatch me away rather than living such a miserable life. Who wants kingdom? Who wants throne? Earned by unrighteous means, all these things are nothing compared to the holy dust of the feet of Rama. But for my love for Rama, who respects you, I would have sent you to the abode of death. I do not see any sin in ruthlessly punishing sinful people like you. Oh, the whole kingdom has misunderstood me by now. Due to my bad *karma* I was born as your son. The only way to put an end to this misery is to put an end to my life itself." Saying thus, Bharata attempted to kill himself by his sword. Sage Vasishta and Shatrughna stopped him from doing so.

Thereafter, Bharata left the palace and along with Sage Vasishta and Shatrughna, came out. There Shatrughna saw the cruel, hunchbacked Manthara, decked with ornaments and new clothes. She was acting as if she was the queen mother of the country. Knowing her to be the cause of all trouble, Shatrughna wanted to send her to the abode of death instantaneously. He knocked her down and pulled her by the tuft of her hair. Manthara cried, "Rama, Rama, if you were here, Rama, you would not have allowed me to be treated like this." When Shatrughna was about to kill her, Bharata said, "Leave the hellish demoness alone, for she has uttered the name of Rama. In the name of our Lord, do not kill her." The angry Shatrughna pointed the sword to her neck and said, "Get out of here, wretched demoness. If you show your face once again anywhere in Ayodhya, I shall bury you alive." The hunchback ran far, far away, crying "Rama, Rama." Never again did anyone hear about her in the whole story of Ramayana!

We should not forget that Manthara had an important part to play in the *avatar* of Sri Rama. But for her, the true glory of Rama and his *avatarhood* would not have been revealed to the world. She was like Judas in the life of Christ Jesus, but for whom the glory of Christ would not have been revealed to the world. Therefore, even though in the story we blame such characters as Manthara and Kaikeyi, they are sent by the Creator for the Cosmic Drama of an *avatar*.

Bharata and Shatrughna, along with Sage Vasishta, came to Rama's mother's palace. Bharata and Shatrughna fell at her feet and Bharata told her, sobbing, "O mother Kausalya, first of all I want to assure you that I am Rama's humble servant. I also want to assure you that this kingdom belongs to Rama and not to me. I swear by the name of Rama that I shall never occupy the throne of Ayodhya, nor shall I sip even a drop of water until I see Rama in the forest. O divine mother, will you kindly bless me and give me enough strength to take all people of Ayodhya to Sri Rama and request Sri Rama to come back to Ayodhya and rule over his kingdom? My agony could never be quenched until I meet Rama and tell all that I have in my heart to my Lord." Hearing the sincere words of Bharata, Kausalya embraced him lovingly and caressed him, saying, "O worthy brother of Rama, you shall bring glory to our race. It is the character, not the position, that brings glory to a man. Your decision is noble. It makes me so happy that you will take us to Rama. That will bring such a great satisfaction to all of our hearts. May God bless you and Shatrughna for this righteous decision that you have taken."

Thereafter, as per the advice of Sage Vasishta, Bharata performed the funeral rites of his father. Raising the corpse from the vat of oil, Bharata offered his prayers to the spirit of his father. "My beloved father, I am an unworthy son but I want to convey to you that I shall do things that will bring peace to your soul. I shall go to the forest, meet Sri Rama, and request him to return to Ayodhya and rule as king. I shall not install myself as the king at all. Please allow me to carry out your obsequies." Thereafter, Sage Vasishta conducted the rites through Bharata and Shatrughna. Sages chanted the *Vedic mantras* and libations were poured. Bharata distributed lots of gold and grains to the priests. After the performance of the funeral rites, Bharata ordered the concerned people to begin constructing roads for their journey to the forest.

Day and night the people worked and constructed the roads. Thousands of people, headed by Bharata, made their way to the bank of the Ganges. Kausalya, Sumitra, and Kaikeyi also followed Bharata to meet Rama. Bharata's devotion to Rama completely converted the heart of Kaikeyi, who realized her folly under the influence of the hunchbacked Manthara.

When they arrived at the bank of the Ganges, Guha, the great devotee of Rama, rebuked Bharata and his troop, thinking that they had come to destroy the peace of the forest and disturb Rama's austerities. Bharata appreciated Guha's devotion to Rama and said, "O Guha, I am an unworthy brother of Sri Ramachandra. Your devotion to my Lord makes all of us more humble, but I want to assure you, we have not come to destroy the peace of the forest or to disturb Sri Rama's forest life. We have come to fall at the feet of Rama for all the wrongs that we have done and request our Lord to come back to Ayodhya to bless us with his rule. I swear this in the name of Rama, whom you love as God. Please take us across the Ganges and tell us of your encounter with Sri Ramachandra."

Thereafter, Guha told all the beautiful conversations which he had with Lord Rama, Lakshmana, and Sita. Hundreds of boatmen, at the instance of Guha, took all people across the Ganges. Chanting Ramanama, Bharata went with his people to Sage Bharadvaja's *ashram*. Sage Bharadvaja blessed him, knowing his devotion to Sri Rama. He offered food and shelter to all and then gave them the directions to Chitrakuta mountain where Sri Rama was dwelling. Bharata decided to leave all his horses and chariots behind and walk the distance to meet Sri Rama. Accompanied by mothers Kausalya, Sumitra, and Kaikeyi, along with Sage Vasishta, Bharata proceeded to Chitrakuta.

When they arrived at Chitrakuta mountain, Bharata cried for joy. "Ram, Ram," he exclaimed, and fell in a trance-like state. After a while, gaining normal consciousness, Bharata cried bitterly, blaming himself and his mother for all the difficulties caused to Rama. Then he was filled with pure devotion and said, "O Chitrakuta mountain, how blessed are you. You have given shelter to *avatar* Rama. O birds that dwell in Chitrakuta, how blessed are ye. You sing the morning songs to my Lord. Even the worms and insects that live in Chitrakuta are blessed. They definitely shall not have rebirth again, for they are blessed by the dwelling of Rama. It would have been better for me if I was born a bird or an insect on this holy mountain than as a brother to Rama to drive him to the forest. O Sage Vasishta, will my beloved Rama forgive me and my mother? Will he give me *darshan* at all? Am I worthy to touch his holy feet? Will the holy sages who dwell here reject me as a sinful one?" He further exclaimed, "O Holy Sage, why should I not have firm faith in my Lord? Why am I doubting in his benevolence? Rama is the ocean of mercy. He will never reject anyone, even though they are his enemies. Whosoever confesses and touches his holy feet is given all blessing; therefore, let me never distrust in Rama's compassion. Let us go." Saying thus, Bharata, that illustrious brother of Sri Rama, walked the distance with all eagerness to meet *avatar* Rama.

Hearing a great noise from a distance, Sri Rama asked Lakshmana to climb a huge tree and find out what was happening. Lakshmana climbed the tree and saw from a distance a large number of people following Bharata and moving in their direction. Hissing with indignation, Lakshmana said, "Rama, give me immediate permission to destroy all these people. Kaikeyi and Bharata are still not satisfied even after occupying Ayodhya. It seems they even want to drive us away from this mountain. With your grace I can destroy all these people in a trice. Allow me to do that." Sri Rama said, "Lakshmana, how can you think such thoughts about Bharata? Don't you know from childhood how devoted he is to me? Even though the sun and the moon change their course, Bharata is not going to change his character. He is most beloved to me and is as steady as this mountain in his devotion to me. Never for a moment doubt in the goodness of Bharata. Hasty action destroys the purpose. Even the cold water should be allowed to be cooler before you drink. In other words, patience and perseverance in such matters is the greatest penance. Get down from that tree. We shall receive Bharata kindly." Lakshmana climbed down from the tree and stood near Sri Ramachandra.

Bharata saw from a distance the Lord of the Universe sitting under the foot of a tree with matted locks and bark garments. The Mother of the Universe, Sita, was shining by his left side and on his right side was standing Lakshmana. The assembly of sages had gathered around Sri Rama. Rama was peaceful and could only be compared to the vast space or unperturbed sublime ocean in his equipoise. From toe to head, devotion to Sri Rama pervaded, and the heart of Bharata welled up as he ran posthaste to the feet of Sri Rama. However he tried, words were choked with supreme devotion, and with folded arms, he fell like a stick at the lotus feet of Rama. For more than half an hour it was only the holy name of 'Rama, Rama, Rama,' engaging his tongue, and he bathed Rama's feet with his tears. That scion of Solar race, Sri Rama, lifted Bharata up and held him in firm embrace as the celestials showered flowers. "Forgive me, forgive me, Rama. Bless me, bless me, Raghava," was the one cry of Bharata. Ramachandra assured him again and again by saying, "There is no cause for such worry. There is no fault to be forgiven. Everything is perfect as per the will of God." Thus he consoled Bharata as an *avatar* should.

Even sages who had renounced all attachments could not help crying at this pure love of God and deep devotion of Bharata. Sages declared: But for such living examples of divine affection, the world would be very poor in realizing the love of God. Making Bharata and Shatrughna feel at home, Sri Rama inquired, thus: "Bharata, did you fulfill the wishes of my father by occupying the throne as king of Ayodhya? How is it that I do not see the insignia of royalty? Why did you come barefoot with all of Ayodhya here to the forest? How is our father? Are you ruling over the kingdom as per *dharma*? Are you punishing the evildoers? Explain to me everything in detail, O my beloved brother." Bharata replied, "Rama, you are God. You know everything. Do not play any of your human *lilas* with me. I am not the ruler of Ayodhya. An ant cannot carry the burden which an elephant alone could carry. You are the Lord of the Universe and you are the king of Ayodhya. That was our father's wish. The whole of Ayodhya has come here to pray at your feet for you to return to Ayodhya and establish the Kingdom of Heaven on earth by your *Rama-rajya*. It makes me sad to give you the bad news of the demise of our beloved father. He died due to the pain of separation from you."

Hearing the news of the death of Dasharatha, Rama, Sita, and Lakshmana were filled with tears by the weight of grief. Thereafter, Sri Rama offered the libations and the funeral cakes to the departed soul of Dasharatha, and all four brothers once again conducted the funeral rites on the bank of the river Mandakini. Collected and composed, they all sat at the *ashram* of Rama. Then Rama said to Bharata and Shatrughna, "Go back, O my beloved brothers, and rule over Ayodhya at my instance. Then alone the word of promise of my father to Kaikeyi will be fulfilled and peace shall dwell in the soul of our father. I cannot come back until I complete my fourteen years of forest life. This is my firm resolve which could never be changed." Bharata decided to go on a hunger strike until Rama returned to Ayodhya. Kaikeyi, full of remorse, begged Rama to forgive her for her wrongdoings and return to Ayodhya. Rama touched the feet of Kaikeyi and confirmed that she was only instrumental in carrying out the Divine Will. Kausalya and Sumitra urged Rama to return to Ayodhya. Sage Vasishta said, "Dasharatha's soul will be happy if he returns to Ayodhya." Another sage, Jabali, insisted that Rama must return to Ayodhya saying that after the death of an individual, there is nothing left known as a soul and Dasharatha having died, had no soul to worry about Rama's return to Ayodhya. Rama admonished Jabali by telling, "O Sage, *Vedas* are the revelations. They declare the soul of man to be eternal. I know you know that. It is only out of love for me you want to decry the *Vedas*, so that I may return to Ayodhya, but I want you to know I have come to establish *Vedic dharma*. Never at any time swerve from the path of *dharma*."

Thereafter Jabali apologized for his wrong statements. Sri Rama very lovingly spoke to Bharata to give up his hunger strike, saying, "My dear Bharata, I know that you are absolutely devoted to me and I want you to know that I love you very much, but it is important to realize that *dharma* is the greatest of all duties. If we swerve from *dharma*, the entire society will fall. We have to uphold *dharma*. Then alone there will be a righteous society. *Dharma* is the power of God which upholds and sustains the individual and society. If you truly love me, my brother, you must go back and rule over the kingdom. For those who love me should keep my commandments." Bharata affirmed, "My Lord, your will is my will. I shall keep your commandments. I am ready to go but I shall not ascend the throne. As your servant I shall serve the people of Ayodhya. I shall throw away all these garments, and wear bark garments, and live like you until you return. If you truly love me, then at least place your sandals on my head. I will carry them as your blessings. I shall install them on the throne and worship them as I worship you. Your sandals will rule over the country and I will be your instrument." Deeply moved by the devotion of Bharata, Sri Rama placed his divine sandals or *padukas* on the head of Bharata. With bark garments and matted locks, Bharata, filled with Rama-consciousness, looked like Rama. Carrying the sandals of Rama on his head, with tears flowing like rivers, Bharata said, "Beloved Rama, Mother Sita, and brother Lakshmana, I am going back to Ayodhya to do the will of my Lord. But behold, Rama, if I do not see you, at the end of the fourteen years of your exile, back in Ayodhya, then this body of mine will be offered to the sacred fires. Keeping this in mind, please come back and give all of us your *darshan*." The sagely assembly, filled with devotion, hailed Bharata and Rama.

Bharata returned to Ayodhya and installed Sri Rama's *padukas* over the throne of Ayodhya in a suburban village called Nandi-grama. Bharata ruled over the country in the name of Rama through the sandals installed on the throne. He never wanted any position other than serving humanity. If everyone keeps this ideal that God is the ruler and we are only the servants of society, the world will be a better place to live.

Bharata lived like an ascetic in Nandi-grama offering all actions to Rama and meditating on his lotus feet. May Bharata's example inspire all of us to serve God with all humility. Here ends the second book, *Ayodhya Kanda*, or the canto of Ayodhya.

BOOK III

ARANYA KANDA

After Bharata and the people of Ayodhya left the forest, Rama decided to move from that mountain to forest Dandaka. As the people of Ayodhya knew his whereabouts, he thought they may frequently visit Chitrakuta and disturb the meditation of the *yogis*. Rama, Lakshmana, and Sita, on their way to Dandaka forest, visited Sage Atri's *ashram*. Sage Atri was one among the Seven Sages known as the mind-born sons of Brahma. His wife, Anasuya, was renowned in three worlds for her chastity and austerity. When the Holy Trinity came to test her chastity, disguising themselves as three priests, she converted them into three children by sprinkling holy water on their bodies. Later, these three children assumed one body with three faces and six arms and became the ever-living Master, Sadguru Dattatreya.

When Rama, Lakshmana, and Sita visited Atri's *ashram*, Sage Atri welcomed them with great devotion. He glorified Avatar Rama for taking the trouble of visiting his ashram to bless all the hermits. Gazing at the transcendental form of Rama, Atri entered into *bhava-samadhi*. Dancing with ecstatic consciousness, Atri sang hymns of praise to Sri Rama. "Salutations to the Lord who is merciful to his devotees. Salutations to the most beautiful Lord, whose feet are the refuge of his votaries. Salutations to the blue-bodied one whose lotus eyes destroy all sins by their glance. Salutations to the Lord of great prowess and of incomparable glory, whose quiver is inexhaustible, and who is the Lord of the three worlds. Adorations to the Lord who is the jewel among the kings of the Solar race, one who has broken the mighty bow of Shiva, enchanter of sages, and destroyer of demons. Prostrations to the Lord, who is saluted by Shiva and Brahma, who is meditated upon as Pure Consciousness, the destroyer of all sins. Salutations to Lakshmi's spouse, the abode of all happiness, the wielder of Kodanda bow. Avatar Rama, salutations. The soul drowning in the ocean of *karma* easily goes across, sitting in the boat of thy Holy Name. You are the wonderful Lord, formless, but who has taken a transcendental form as *Jagadguru*. You are realized in deep meditation. Lord Rama, even though you are the Transcendental Reality, you are easily attainable through *bhakti*. You are the wish-yielding tree of your votaries. O Lord of incomparable beauty, dazzling spouse of Sita, bless me with pure devotion to your lotus feet." Hearing this great prayer, Rama blessed Atri, revealing His Transcendental Nature.

Thereafter, Rama brought Atri to normal consciousness. Atri offered him fruits and milk. At the insistence of Atri, Rama sent Sita inside the hermitage to meet Atri's wife, Anasuya. When these two great women met, there was a spiritual blessing to the entire universe and to the glory of womanhood. Immortal Anasuya blessed Sita with the following words: "Sita, renouncing Ayodhya and all its luxuries, you have followed Rama to the forest. This shows your greatness, that before your husband, nothing is more important to you. You are a jewel among women and your name will be perpetually on the lips of millions. But Sita, there may come so many difficulties and tests in your life, come what may, do not swerve from the path of your purity. I am fixing this flower to your braid, which will never fade, and I apply this ointment to your body, by the virtue of which you will always remain hale and hearty. Accept also these jewels, O beautiful spouse of Rama." Sita received the gifts given by Anasuya and thanked her for such a blessing. She promised her that she would maintain her *dharma* at any cost, under all circumstances. Receiving their blessings, Rama, Lakshmana, and Sita proceeded to Dandaka forest. Old Anasuya, with her white hair and white brows, filled with a radiant aura, accompanied by Sage Atri, followed them for a little distance and bid them farewell.

Rama entered Dandaka forest. Sages who were living there were very happy to receive the three of them. As they were moving in the forest, suddenly there was a tempestuous wind. A demon called Viradha siezed Sita and carried her away on his shoulders. Standing in the sky, he challenged Rama and Lakshmana. Sita cried with agony at separation from Rama. Receiving the blessings of Rama, Lakshmana pierced the breast of the demon with his sharp arrow. Even though the demon vomited blood, he gave a clamor and burst into laughter, saying, "Hey Rama and Lakshmana, I am invulnerable to any weapon. Such is the boon I have been given from the creator, Brahma." Rama was angry and he struck the demon with his sharp arrows. The demon fell on the ground and Sita was released from his grip by Lakshmana. The demon rose again and carried away Rama and Lakshmana, leaving Sita on the ground. Sita was very much afraid the demon might harm her beloved Rama and Lakshmana. Showing the gesture of fearlessness, both brothers cut off the two arms of the demon, whereby the demon fell on the ground, like a mountain struck by the thunderbolt. Seeing the demon invulnerable, Rama asked Lakshmana to dig a pit to bury him alive. Then the demon spoke to them the truth of his past life.

"Rama and Lakshmana, I was a celestial musician named Tumburu. Due to a wrong I did to Ramba, the celestial nymph, Kubera, the god of wealth, punished me with this monstrous shape, to wander in this forest disturbing the sages. At my prayer, Kubera softened the curse by telling, 'When you recognize Rama, the *avatar*, vanquished by him, you will assume your original form and return to the higher heavens.' By your grace, O Rama, I realize your greatness now. You are Lord Vishnu incarnated in a human body. Salutations to you. By your grace I am delivered from this monstrous form." Saying thus, he gave up the ghost and ascended to the celestial region. Lakshmana buried his body in the pit.

Sage Sharabhanga

Slaying demon Viradha, Sri Rama, Lakshmana, and Sita walked in the great forest. There were various great sages performing austerities and meditation for years. To give them *darshan* and to shower his grace, Avatar Rama decided to visit their *ashrams*.

There was a Sage named Sharabhanga. He was a life celibate, constantly meditating on God. The power of his austerity was so much that Indra, the lord of the first heaven, was waiting with his celestial aerial car to take him to the higher *lokas*, but Sharabhanga told him, "Indra, go away. I do not care to live in any higher *loka* when Heavenly Father Vishnu is walking on earth as Rama. I want to have his *darshan* which brings *bhakti* and *mukti*." Hearing these words of Sharabhanga, Indra left for his heavenly abode.

After a while, the old sage, Sharabhanga, had the *darshan* of Sri Rama. He rolled at the feet of the Lord with great devotion and praised him thus: "Rama, compassionate Rama, Rama, Sitarama, you are the swan visible to Shiva in his mind's lake. To smear my body by the pollen of your feet, I have been waiting, rejecting Indra's aerial car and Brahmaloka. My whole life was spent in deep meditation for your *darshan*. Even though I attained Supreme Consciousness, still I was not satisfied until I saw you in this transcendental form. All *sadhana* culminates in your grace. *Yoga*, fire-sacrifice, austerity, repetition of the Holy Name, are insignificant before your true love. May you live in my heart forever, O infinite Lord." Sri Rama blessed him with pure love. Thereafter, Sharabhanga prepared his own funeral pyre and sat on it in lotus posture and asked Rama to light the fire with his own hand, which Rama did. Gazing at the transcendental form of Rama, Sharabhanga left his body, by breaking open the tenth aperture at the top of the head; his soul merged in Supreme God. His body was reduced to ashes. Celestials showered flowers on Rama. Sita and Lakshmana glorified Rama as they walked with him to the next *ashram*.

Sage Suteekshna

The living sages during the time of Rama recognized him as the *avatar* of the time. According to the *Upanishads*, one who has transcendental beauty, inexhaustible energy, universal wisdom, the power to heal and bless humanity, the power of renunciation, the power of all-embracing love and forgiveness is an *avatar* of the Lord. Rama had all these qualifications and innumerable other divine virtues as well. He decided to visit Sage Suteekshna's *ashram* to bless him.

The great Sage Suteekshna saw in his meditation beautiful Lord Sri Rama appearing in his heart. His mind became absorbed at the feet of the Lord, and filled with great ecstasy, he entered into different moods of mystical experiences. He stood up with uplifted arms and felt that Rama was coming on a road and began running in that direction. His eyes being filled with tears of joy, he couldn't even see the way. Sri Rama wanted to see his devotion to him and stood behind a tree. Sage Suteekshna sang the name of Rama and fell at times with ecstatic consciousness, rolling on the ground feeling the pangs of separation. Experiencing horripilation at times, perspiring at times, his whole body trembled with deep devotion to the Lord. Finally, he sat firmly, absorbed in deep meditation seeing the transcendental form of God in his heart. Even though Sri Rama himself came and stood in front of him, Suteekshna would not open his eyes, due to the divine form which he was enjoying in his heart. Suddenly Sri Rama disappeared from his heart and then alone the sage opened his eyes and saw in his presence the sky-colored Rama with Sita and his brother Lakshmana. Out of deep devotion, he fell at the feet of the Lord and Rama, with his long arms, held him in his firm embrace. For a few minutes, Suteekshna experienced supramental bliss.

Requesting Sri Rama to come to his *ashram*, Suteekshna, along with other sages, prepared everything to worship the feet of the Lord. There, according to the scriptural injunction, they worshipped the feet of the Lord and praised him with the following prayer: "Salutations to Sri Rama, walking with matted locks and bark garments, holding the bow Kodanda and carrying the inexhaustible quiver. Let me meditate always on that blue-colored Rama. I surrender to Rama who is Vishnu. He is like a fire to the forest of attachment. He is like the sun in blossoming the heart's lotus of saints. He is like a lion in destroying the elephants of demons. Salutations, salutations to Rama.

"I salute unto him who is the young swan, floating in the mind's lake of Shiva. He is the moon that brings happiness to the eyes of Sita which are like Chakora birds. I meditate on that full-moon face and lotus petal-like eyes. I salute unto him who is like the eagle that destroys the serpents of doubts; one who calms the mind by merely meditating on his name; one who delights the celestials and destroys the rebirth. To him I salute; on him I meditate. Salutations unto him who is both formless and with form. One who is difficult to attain even by the *jnana yogis*. I salute unto him who is pure, almighty, of illimitable powers. One who has incarnated to relieve the earth of its burden. My salutations unto him who is like the wish-yielding tree to his devotees, the resting place of his votaries, the presence of whom drives away anger, greediness, arrogance, and lust. One who is the bridge over the ocean of *samsara*. Salutations, salutations to my Lord Rama. I salute unto him who is the abode of all strength and power, one who is realized through the sacred *dharma*, one whose Holy Name destroys all evil. I know the indestructible Lord is all-pervading, yet he is the indwelling spirit in the heart of everybody. May that Lord with Sita and Lakshmana sit on the throne of my heart forever. Those who know, alone know, that he is both the Lord with form and without, the indwelling spirit and the incarnate Lord, king of Ayodhya. Let that Lord sit in my heart forever. He is my master; I am his servant." Hearing this prayer of Sage Suteekshna, Lord Rama was pleased and blessed him with pure love and peace.

Sage Agastya

Sage Suteekshna directed Rama and his people to Sage Agastya's *ashram*. As per his direction, they arrived at Agastya's hermitage. Rama said, "O Sita and Lakshmana, look at the peace of this great *ashram*. It seems in all seasons the trees yield fruits here. Sun is afraid of bringing scorching heat here and therefore it is cool. Birds are chanting the *Vedas*. Nature is the stage. When the birds sing, the peacock dances, spreading its rich plumage. Serpents come out of their abodes and nod their hoods and dance on their tails. The breeze is fragrant and humming bees hum the *mantras*. Elephants sweep the *ashram* grounds, and tiger and cows, mice and cats, lion and deer, play together. Lakshmana, I will tell you the greatness of this Master Agastya as I have heard the story from other Masters.

"Lakshmana and Sita, long ago two demons named Ilvala and Vatapi lived here in this forest and were terror to the sages. Ilvala would disguise himself as a sage and invite saintly people to his home for a feast. The cruel demon would prepare the dish by the flesh of his brother Vatapi who would assume the form of a goat, and feed it to the ascetics. After they were fed, Ilvala would call him, 'Vatapi, come out,' and Vatapi would burst the stomachs of the sages, killing all of them, and he used to become whole once again by some *tamasic* magic power. They used to enjoy this hideous prank everyday. Hundreds of sages were killed this way by them, until Sage Agastya arrived there. Inviting that great sage, Ilvala fed him with Vatapi's flesh. As usual, he called Vatapi to come out and the great Sage Agastya completely digested him by the power of his *yoga* and said, 'Vatapi is dead and gone. He will never come out again.' When Ilvala came upon him with anger, Agastya consumed him with a single glance."

Esoterically, this story could be taken to mean the pairs of opposites that bother even the *yogis* were digested by Sage Agastya, one who has transcended the duality.

Rama continued, "Lakshmana, once it so happened, Mount Vindhya, competing with other mountains, began growing in size, covering the skies. The peaks of that mountain never allowed the light of the sun to reach the earth. Sages and celestials complained to Sage Agastya. Thereupon the great Sage went to Vindhya mountain. Seeing the immortal Master, Vindhya mountain, like a good disciple, bent its head to the feet of Agastya. Immediately, the Sage ordered the mountain to remain in that bent position forever and never to raise its head. The Vindhya mountain had to behave, as per the mandate of Master Agastya. Such is the power of *yoga* and meditation, O Lakshmana."

Esoterically this means that a *yogi* of realization will have complete control over nature.

Describing the glory of Sage Agastya, Rama, with his spouse and brother, entered into Agastya's *ashram*. Shining like the sun, surrounded by his disciples, the great sage came to receive Rama. To show reverence to the *gurus*, Rama, Lakshmana and Sita bowed before Agastya and Agastya received them very warmly. He embraced Rama and spoke to him with great reverence, "Rama, I know that you are an incarnation of Lord Vishnu. You have come to establish *dharma*. Taking this human form, making Kaikeyi an excuse, you have come to the forest to fulfill your *avatarhood*. Rama, when you took away Vishnu's bow from the hand of Parashurama, he told you that was the bow you shall use during the destruction of the ten-headed demon, Ravana. You gave that bow to Varuna, the god of water, to preserve it for you, and he had handed it over to me to give you on your arrival. Receive this celestial bow. As an incarnation of Vishnu, you alone are entitled to hold this bow. Here are some infallible arrows and missiles. They will be of immense use to you during the destruction of demons. Please accept this, O Rama, the Abode of Divine Virtue." As Agastya offered the bow of Vishnu, Rama received it respectfully and held it by his hand. Then the true nature of Rama as Vishnu was revealed to Sage Agastya and Agastya saluted Rama with joined palms and offered the following prayer.

"Rama, Sitarama, who am I before you? It is only by your grace that I was given this opportunity to serve you. Hey, Prabho, your *maya* is this universal tree. Endless worlds are like fruits. Innumerable creatures are like the worms inside the fruits who know not either inside or outside. They are born, they grow, and they die inside the fruit. The god of death is the one who eats all the fruits and even the god of death is always afraid of you, who is the destroyer of death and bestower of immortality. Such Lord of the universe thou art, appearing to me in such simple human form. Do not delude me by your *maya*. May I see your light always, hey Rama. Every pore of your body in this transcendental form is the source of endless universes. I see it by your grace. May you remain always in my heart with Lakshmana and Sita. Association with those who love you and true devotion to your lotus feet, these are the only two boons I pray for. Accept me as your humble servant forever." Saying thus, Agastya saluted Rama and showed him the way to the most beautiful forest retreat called Panchavati and requested Rama to stay there. He said, "Rama, so many sages meditate on you in the forest of Panchavati. Bless them with your presence." Sri Rama, blessing Sage Agastya, made his way to the beautiful forest of Panchavati.

Shoorpanakha

As per Sage Agastya's instruction, Rama stayed in Panchavati very happily. Ten years were spent in meeting the holy sages, giving them *darshan*, discussing the *Vedas*, and observing austerities.

One day as Rama and Sita were sitting quietly and Lakshmana was writing over every tree 'Sri Rama Jaya Rama Jaya Jaya Rama' mantra, there came Ravana's younger sister, Shoorpanakha, the demoness. The demoness was drunk and was very ugly with bloodshot eyes. Ravana, the ten-headed demon, had made all arrangements for her stay in that forest, keeping fourteen thousand military men headed by three demons named Khara, Dushana, and Trishiras. They were all there for her protection. She roamed and wandered throughout the forest, killing and eating ascetics and animals.

No sooner she saw the strong, blue-bodied Rama, then and there she fell in love with him and approached him shamelessly. By the power of magic, she could take any form she liked and therefore, she took the form of a lovely woman and came to Sri Rama. She spoke to Rama, saying, "O beautiful ascetic, who are you? You are most welcome to stay in this forest or in my home. I am your host. This forest belongs to me. I have never seen in my life anyone more beautiful than you. Many people tried to marry me but I rejected everyone. I am well-guarded by fourteen thousand military men. I am a thousand times more beautiful than the woman who is sitting by your side. Why should an ascetic have a woman by his side? It seems you are a disguised prince. Whatever it is, I love you and I want you to marry me without any delay. You might have heard about the great Ravana, the ruler of Lanka. Know it for sure that I am his sister, Shoorpanakha. I have two other brothers named Kumbhakarna and Vibhishana. What is the use of living with this poor, thin woman? You can move at will with me and enjoy this life. If this woman is a problem, I can just eat her and solve your problem. First of all, tell me who you are and who is the other man there and who is this woman sitting by your side."

Rama was amazed at her untimely and uncouth words. Sita was terribly afraid and held Rama's hand. Rama gave her assurance through his loving eyes and even though he was always serious, he wanted to amuse himself in such a situation. Rama said, "O Shoorpanakha, I am very thankful to you for welcoming us to stay in this forest. I wish I could fulfill your desires, but unfortunately I have married this woman, whose name is Sita. Therefore, it is impossible for me to marry another woman. But one thing I will advise you. That young man there is my younger brother, Lakshmana. Fortunately, he has not brought his wife with him. I think you have every chance of having him as your husband, provided you enchant him."

The demoness Shoorpanakha was very happy. She went to Lakshmana and said to him, "O beautiful young man, I love you and you alone. You are so beautiful and I am more beautiful than you. We really match one another in every respect. Be happy with me by marrying me." Lakshmana was very angry. When he looked at Rama, Rama gave him the eye signal to take it as an amusement. Lakshmana understood, and turning toward the woman, he said, "O lovely woman, I would have really accepted your proposal to marry you but unfortunately I am not free, being a slave to that Rama. You will not be enjoying your life happily with a slave like me. If you insist, I am sure Rama may marry you. Why don't you go back and tell him that you want to marry him and him alone."

Again Shoorpanakha returned to Rama and told him that she never liked the other man and she wanted to marry only Rama. Again Sita was afraid. Rama held her hand and assured her with his loving smile that there was no cause for fear. Turning toward the demoness, Rama said, "O beautiful woman, Lakshmana is adamant. He just wanted to see whether you love him wholeheartedly. Just to test you he has sent you back to me. This time you should go back to him and tell him of your total devotion to him. Then he may agree. Having Sita by my side, I cannot marry you." Shoorpanakha again went back to Lakshmana and Lakshmana sent her back again. Now Shoorpanakha understood the two men were playing a trick on her and she thought, "If I finish Sita, then Rama will agree to marry me." Thinking thus, she rushed toward Sita, taking her fierce, demoness form and Sita cried, "Hey Rama, hey Lakshmana." Enraged at this, the powerful Lakshmana rushed toward the demoness and chopped off her nose and ears and drove her away.

Uttering a loud wail and carrying her nose and ears on her palms, the ugly looking ogress ran to her camp in the forest. She complained of her agony to Khara, the commander-in-chief of the fourteen thousand military men. Mutilated and disgraced, she told her story in a twisting way. She said, "O Khara, Dushana, and all my brothers, as usual I was roaming in the forest. Two young men who were brothers saw me and perhaps fell in love with me, and eager to marry me, they approached me. When I rejected their offer, one of them maimed me and drove me away. They have a lovely woman by their side whom they call Sita. This really is an insult to all of you and my brother Ravana that I should be punished like this by ordinary ascetics. They should be killed immediately." Hearing these words of Shoorpanakha, Khara gave orders to Dushana to take the military men to handle the situation. With fourteen thousand demons, Dushana and Trishiras came to the hermitage where Rama was dwelling.

Keeping Sita under the protection of Lakshmana, Rama faced all the demons single-handedly. When he twanged the Kodanda bow, its tumultuous noise broke the heart of the demons. The innumerable shafts discharged by the demons were all consumed by the fire arrow of Rama. The proud army of Dushana fell like moths in the blazing fire of Rama's arrow. Among the eighteen bells which were decked to Kodanda bow, only a few bells sounded as Rama destroyed the fourteen thousand military men. When all eighteen bells ring, Rama can destroy all the fourteen worlds by his unlimited power.

Dushana and Trishiras fought Rama gallantly. To their utter amazement, they saw that if Rama discharges one arrow, when it reaches the enemy, it becomes thousands of arrows; and until it pulls the soul out of the body of the enemy, it never returns. After the destruction, the arrow returns back to Rama. So all their magic arrows utterly failed before Rama. Pulling the string of his bow with the arrow to his ear, Rama discharged a powerful shaft which pierced the bosom of Dushana, who fell dead instantaneously. Like the God of destruction, bringing an untimely cataclysm, Rama danced over the bodies of the demons as Trishiras fought with him ferociously. Breaking his chariot to pieces with his sharp arrows, Rama made him stand on his legs on earth and cut off his three heads, one after another. With a small army, the commander-in-chief, Khara, rushed forth to destroy Rama. The demon played different tricks through his magical power, assuming different forms and hitting with different weapons at Rama. The Almighty God, Rama, set his magic at naught and said, "O terrible demon, terror of the sages and saints, your death is at hand." Saying thus, Rama hit him with a very powerful missile. That weapon destroyed the mace and the sword of the demon and clove his bow into two. Another arrow sprang from the bow of Rama like lightning, which cut off the head of the cruel demon and killed him. There was a grand festival in the skies. *Devas* showered flowers. Celestial nymphs danced as *gandharvas* sang. Avatar Rama began fulfilling his pledge to the *devas* of the destruction of the demons and protection of the pious. Sages of Panchavati glorified Sri Rama. It was clear to people that Rama was no ordinary man, but Lord Vishnu in human form.

Esoterically, this means that innumerable demoniac, dark powers could be shattered to pieces by the light of Truth.

Having her entire army destroyed, Shoorpanakha rushed back to Lanka and came and fell at the feet of Ravana. In the midst of a great assembly, Shoorpanakha narrated her sad story to Ravana. "O Ravana," she cried, "you are known as the ruler over the three worlds by your prowess. *Devas* are afraid of you, but what is the use when your sister is mutilated this way by ordinary human beings? Through no fault of mine, struck by my beauty, that Rama and Lakshmana wanted to marry me, and when I denied, they insulted me and cut off my nose and ears. O Ravana, I know how you should punish them. Rama has a beautiful wife. Very few can surpass her beauty. I know you have the most beautiful women of the world as your queens. I know you have all the wealth of the world but what is the use? If only you could have Sita as your queen, all that which you have carries meaning. Once Sita is carried away by you, then Rama and Lakshmana will die tortuously by the pangs of separation from her. To see you happy makes me happy, even though my limbs are cut off. Please take a decision today to carry away Sita from Rama."

Hearing the words of his sister, Ravana decided to abduct Sita. Accordingly, he flew in his aerial car called Pushpaka Vimana and reached his uncle Mareecha's *ashram*. Now the reader may remember who Mareecha is. In the first book of Ramayana, when Rama was taken by Sage Vishwamitra to his *ashram*, the two sons of demoness Tataka disturbed the fire-sacrifice. Then, at the instance of Vishwamitra, Rama killed Subahu and made Mareecha fly across the seven seas by his arrows and fall somewhere in a forest near Lanka. From that time onward, Mareecha meditated on Rama, building a hermitage on that spot. This demon was an uncle of Ravana and Ravana wanted to use him for his own purpose.

Seeing Ravana entering his hermitage, Mareecha welcomed him and asked him the cause of his arrival. Ravana answered, "Listen, O Mareecha. I need help from you. My sister Shoorpanakha was insulted and maimed by Lakshmana and Rama. To add to this, Rama also destroyed fourteen thousand military men along with Khara, Dushana and Trishiras. I want to retaliate by carrying off Rama's wife Sita. In this I seek your help."

Hearing the name Rama, Mareecha fell unconscious

for some time. Ravana asked the reason for such behavior. Mareecha replied, "O Ravana, I don't think you know Rama and his prowess. Rama is the one who broke Shiva's bow, which you could not, and married Sita. Your sister, Shoorpanakha, is of such courage and strength, yet you know that she was mutilated. Just now I heard from you that the three commanders of your army with fourteen thousand people were destroyed by Rama single-handedly. Why do you not understand that Rama is no ordinary man? I have had a great experience with the arrow of Rama. I believed that I was the strongest man of my time, but one arrow of Rama tossed me across the seven oceans, to this place. After that experience, Rama's name became my *mantra*. I am terribly afraid of him and revere him as God. O Ravana, whosoever has given you this wrong advice of abducting Sita, did it with ignorance. Even according to the holy scriptures, to hanker after another's wife is highly sinful. You are definitely bringing the destruction of your race if you take such a wrong decision. I implore you not to take such a dangerous decision."

Ravana was very angry. He said, "Mareecha, breathes there anyone on earth or anywhere who can face this mighty Ravana in battle? Know you not that I have vanquished all the *devas* and have made Indra and other guardian deities my servants? Know you not I have lifted Kailasa mountain and obtained the grace of Shiva? Know you not that there is nothing impossible for me in all the three worlds? I cannot bear the insult Lakshmana has done to my sister and the destruction of my military men by Rama. I want to avenge myself by abducting Sita. All that I need is for you to obey my command. Let both of us go in my aerial car to Panchavati. There I want you to take the form of a golden deer, with silver spots all over the body. You should enchant Sita and she should ask her dear Rama to bring this deer. Seeing Rama and Lakshmana away from the *ashram* in search of the deer, I will easily carry Sita away in my aerial car to Lanka. From the time I have heard about her beauty, I have been waiting for the opportunity to bring her to Lanka."

Mareecha said, "Ravana, your ten heads shall not be safe by this decision. Destruction of your family and your race is at hand. Sita is Divine Mother; Rama is Heavenly Father. He has incarnated to destroy the wicked and protect the good. I speak from my experience and I warn you again to desist from such an evil action."

Hearing these words of Mareecha, Ravana lifted his fist and rushed toward his uncle, "O Mareecha, I am going to kill you right now. You are extolling my enemy and discouraging my purpose. Let me send you to the abode of death." Mareecha said, "O Ravana, better for me to die in the hands of Rama than to die by your sinful hand. At least let me have the *darshan* of Rama at the time of my death." Saying thus, Mareecha started with Ravana.

Both of them flew across the ocean in the aerial car and arrived in Panchavati. Mareecha, by his magical powers, converted himself into a golden stag. He came to Sita while she was bathing in a beautiful lake. Rama and Lakshmana were in the nearby hermitage. Sita saw the reflection of the golden deer in the water. Fascinated by the beauty of the deer she turned her face and saw that indescribably beautiful stag standing there. She came up to catch it but it ran away from her. Sita again went into the water, and the deer once again came and attracted her mind. Sita completed her bath and dressing herself neatly, came to catch the golden deer. Sita saw the exquisite beauty of the deer. Its golden skin had the pictures of different flowers and gems. It wandered here and there and and whenever Sita tried to catch it, it disappeared somewhere in the forest. When she became frustrated, it would come to pull her hair by its mouth. Finally, Sita called her dear Rama and said, "My dear, look at that deer. It has endeared itself to me and I don't think I can stay without it. Please come quickly; otherwise, some hunter may take it away."

Hearing these words of Sita, Rama and Lakshmana came running. They were suspicious of the extraordinarily beautiful deer. Lakshmana said, "O Divine Mother, this is no ordinary deer of the forest. This is definitely a demon in this form." Sita said, "Lakshmana, why are you unnecessarily suspicious? This is a lay excuse that you cannot bring it to me. It is really a very beautiful deer. Rama, you two brothers many a time go hunting leaving me alone. I feel so lonely in the *ashram*. If you could bring me this deer, I will play with it and it will play with me. Then I need not bother you about my loneliness. Please do catch this deer for me. Look, it is pulling my hair. It already loves me so much. Rama, look at its color. Anyone who has eyes cannot help appreciating it. Please bring it for me. Rama, perhaps after our forest life, we may take it to Ayodhya. All will be happy."

Both Rama and Lakshmana tried their best in convincing her not to be attached to the golden deer and they tried to convince her that it must be some magical trick of a demon but she would not listen. Rama knew that something was going to happen. The power of destiny is such that all are carried away by its bewitching smile. Rama said, "Lakshmana, please be vigilant and guard Sita from all sides. I will go to fulfill her wishes. Suppose this is the trick of a demon, then I shall kill him." Lakshmana said, "Rama, why should you go for such a small thing? I can kill the demon or bring the deer, if it is truly a deer." Rama said, "Lakshmana, I think I have to do this myself. Please take care of Sita. As some demoniacal trick is involved, anything may happen at any time. No matter what happens, do not leave Sita alone, please." Lakshmana agreed.

Rama began chasing the golden deer. Appearing and disappearing, hiding and manifesting, stopping awhile and taking a leap, the stag gave Rama a difficult time.

Rama tried varieties of ways of catching it but it escaped and took him away, far away from his hermitage. Seeing that his efforts went ineffectual in catching the deer alive, Rama decided to kill the deer and pulled the string of his Kodanda bow. Now demon Mareecha knew that his end was near. Now that deer, gazing at Rama's beauty, joined its palms and meditated on Rama. As the sharp arrow of Rama struck the deer, Mareecha died with a cry, imitating the voice of Rama, "O Lakshmana, Ah Sita, O Lakshmana, Ah Sita." The voice of Mareecha reached Sita's *ashram*. It was exactly like the voice of Rama. Sita was very disturbed. She called Lakshmana and said, "Lakshmana, don't you hear the voice of my beloved Rama? As you predicted, this is the trick of a demon who took the form of the golden deer. Now I am afraid that Rama is in trouble. Delay no more. Rush to Rama and protect him from the demon." Lakshmana said, "O Holy Mother, I need not tell you that Rama is invincible. Rama is God. How can any demon harm him? I think it is again the demon's trick of simulating the voice of Rama and trying to confuse us. Please hold your peace. Let us chant the name of Rama and everything will be all right." But Sita said, "Lakshmana, I know my husband's voice clearer than you. I know that Rama is invincible but I feel he needs help and therefore, he has cried, calling you and me by our names. I don't think any demon can imitate the voice of Rama. Delay no more, my son. Hurry, please!" Lakshmana said, "O Divine Mother, I cannot go, even though I want to at your behest. Rama has specifically assigned this duty to me of protecting you from the demons. I am sorry I cannot carry out your orders. Rama's order binds me and I must stay here to take care of you. I want to again convince you, Rama shall slay the demon and return to us very soon." Sita lost her patience and became angry.

She said, "Lakshmana, when your elder brother is in imminent danger, despite my repeated request, you decide not to go. I am positive that Rama is in danger. Posing yourself as an obedient servant, you followed us from Ayodhya only with a crooked plan in your evil mind. O wretched one. It seems you want to see the death of my husband so that you may rule over me. Stay not even for a minute in my presence. Get out of my sight." Hearing these words of Sita, Lakshmana turned his face, suffering an untold misery. He wished the sky to fall on his head or the earth to open its mouth and devour him. He chanted a few times, "Rama, Rama, Rama," plugging his ears. Joining his palms to Sita, he respectfully spoke to her saying, "O Holy Mother, the time is bad. The destiny is powerful; therefore, words unworthy of you are emerging from your lips. Never even in my dream did I think of anything such as that which you spoke. I swear in the name of Rama, I have come only to serve you and Rama. Let all the guardian deities be the witness to this fact. Much against my will, I will go to please you but I know some danger is ahead. I shall put a demarcating line with my arrow, writing the name of Rama on it so that no demon can enter beyond the line to disturb you; but I pray you, Mother, do not cross this boundary line I have drawn." Saying thus, Lakshmana, that immortal devotee of Rama, ran in the direction of the reverberating sound.

Abduction of Sita

Ravana, who was waiting for this opportunity, disguised himself as a monk and came to Sita's *ashram*. Clad in saffron clothes, humming some *mantra*, he stood near the *ashram*. Sita came out upon hearing the *mantras*, thinking that a sage had come to bless her. Now Ravana's eyes fell on her and he was struck by her beauty, but he immediately closed his eyes, posing himself as an ascetic.

He held his begging bowl stretched out for alms. Sita offered him fruits while standing within the line drawn by Lakshmana. Ravana said, "O chaste lady, why are you hesitating in offering the alms to a man who has renounced the world? The offering becomes futile when it is not offered reverentially and fearlessly. So please come forward properly and offer the fruits; otherwise, I shall go away." Sita was afraid that he may utter a curse and this may bring more agony to her. Despite Lakshmana's warning, carried away by destiny, Sita crossed the boundary line and offered the alms. Demon Ravana knew that if he touched her, he would be reduced to ashes by the power of her chastity, so he lifted the very earth where she was standing and revealed his true form. He said, "Sita, I am the lord of Lanka. I tried to marry you in your father's court but I could not lift the Shiva bow on that day; consequently, I took a pledge to carry you away some time and now I am happy that you are with me. Let us go to Lanka where I will make you my queen."

Saying thus, the demon took the piece of earth along with Sita, in his aerial car, and flew away. Sita cried aloud, "O Rama, O Lakshmana, what happened to me today? It is my desire which has brought this calamity. I should have listened to the words of Rama. I should have obeyed Lakshmana's words. Cruel fate overwhelmed me and bewildered me. Rama, protect me. Lakshmana, save me from this demon." Turning toward the demon, Sita said, "O lustful wretch, you will be destroyed by the arrow of Rama. It will not be safe for you to do this sinful action. Leave me in my hermitage." Ravana burst into laughter and said, "Sita, forget that beggar Rama. I am all-powerful and no one can take you away from me anymore. Be quiet and become my queen." Sita cried loudly and helplessly. She appealed to every tree, bird, flower, sun, moon, stars, ocean, and the entire nature saying, "O nature spirits, please tell Sri Rama that the demon carried me away, that I am in utter helplessness, that Rama should rescue me from this misery."

Jatayu

There was a powerful bird named Jatayu who was always meditating on Rama. He heard the cry of Sita from Pushpaka Vimana and decided to help Sita. That huge eagle, chanting the name of Rama, flew across the sky and stopped the ten-headed demon, saying, "O ten-headed worm, I am going to punish you for taking away Rama's wife. Know you not that Rama is the Lord of the Universe and Sita the Universal Mother? I shall never give way until you conquer me in this aerial fight." This was really a challenge to demon Ravana, who tried to escape, but the king of eagles attacked his heads, taking away his diadems. He hurt him in such a way with his claws that a fierce battle ensued. It seemed as if two mountains were fighting. Ravana began bleeding, his face and bosom torn by the sharp claws of the bird. Seeing that he could not win through a righteous battle with the bird, Ravana devised an evil plan. He said, "O Jatayu, if you go on fighting, there is no end. To test our might, both of us should reveal the sacred spots in our body where our life energy is stored. Then we could see one another's might." To deceive the bird, Ravana said his life energy was stored in his toes. The bird, however, spoke the truth, that his life current was stored in his wings. During the ensuing fight, Jatayu tried to attack Ravana's toes with his beak, and taking this opportunity, Ravana cut off his wings. Then the great eagle fell like a mountain hit by lightning, chanting "Sitaram, Sitaram." Sita could not bear this sight. She blessed the bird saying, "O Jatayu, you are my true friend and my father. People will remember your sacrifice for the sake of *dharma*. May your soul never leave the body until you have the *darshan* of Rama."

The cruel demon Ravana flew across the ocean carrying Sita away, who constantly cried, remembering her Rama. As she was flying, she saw a number of huge monkeys on the Rishyamuka mountain. Tearing the end of her *sari*, she put all the jewels given by Anasuya, and packing them properly in that piece of cloth, she hurled them over that mountain. The monkeys handed them to their chief, Sugriva, who preserved them carefully. Thereafter, Ravana took her to Lanka and tried to tempt her in a number of ways. Seeing her devotion to Rama, Ravana kept her in his most beautiful Ashoka grove at the foot of a beautiful tree called Shimshupa under heavy guard. He tried to tempt her in every way showing his palace, wealth, offering her ornaments, rich food, etc., but Sita never touched anything, and told Ravana that all his riches paled into insignificance in front of Rama's love. Sita meditated on Rama night and day without eating or drinking.

As Rama was returning in the forest, after the destruction of Mareecha, his left eye began to throb and he thought evil portents were ahead. He suspected that Mareecha's cry, imitating his voice, might have confused Lakshmana and Sita and was eager to rush to the hermitage to hear of the safety of Sita. On his way, he met Lakshmana, who was sobbing and crying. Rama said, "Lakshmana, how could you leave Sita alone in the hermitage? Didn't I tell you, my son, that you should not leave Sita alone? Repeatedly I insisted that demons may bring harm to her. Lakshmana, you who were the most obedient brother, how could you think of disobeying my words? My heart is troubled that great harm might come to Sita before we reach the hermitage. Tell me, my son, why did you leave her alone?" Lakshmana said with faltering words, "Sri Rama, you know I am your obedient servant but today, much against my will, I had to transgress your words. Mother Sita abused me by saying that my intention was absolutely wrong in following you to the forest. She suspected that I was after her. She ordered me to leave the hermitage without delay as we heard a cry imitating your voice. Even though I repeatedly told the Divine Mother it was a demon's trick, still she did not believe me. All my efforts were in vain. Forgive me, my God, my Master, and my brother. Rama, please forgive me."

Rama and Lakshmana came running to the hermitage. Rama called Sita loudly by name but there was no response. Rama ran inside the hermitage but could not find Sita. Both of them went around the *ashram* but there was no trace of her. Remembering her divine face, Rama lamented at her loss. "Sita, where are you? Even though I repeatedly requested you not to leave Ayodhya, not to come with me to the forest, you insisted on coming. Even though both Lakshmana and I told you in clear terms that the golden stag was a demon's magic, you never believed us and you insisted in my going to bring it for you. Out of attachment and affection for you, I went chasing the golden deer, appointing Lakshmana to take care of you. O Maithili, you unnecessarily suspected Lakshmana's sincerity, sent him out much against his will, and brought calamity on yourself. O Janaki, where shall I search for you now? Are you hiding somewhere to test my love for you? If so, please come out wherever you are. Delay no more. I cannot live without you. Sita, Sita, where are you?"

Saying thus, Rama again fainted. After a while, gathering his senses, Rama asked the entire nature to tell him about Sita. "O trees, tell me where my beloved Sita is. O birds, your sad songs add apprehension in my heart. Tell me the direction in which Sita went. O river Godavari, be compassionate to me in telling me the location where Sita is hiding. O creepers and flowers, Sita loved you so much. Please convey her message. O herd of deer, I am sure you know the direction in which Sita has gone. Why are you all silent? Why should nature, so full of life, be dumb to me today? Oh, there is no one more unfortunate than I. Lakshmana, throughout my life I suffer. When I was a boy, you and I were taken away from our parents by Sage Vishwamitra. Then we had to face terrible demons with whom we fought. Then I had to walk along with you to Janaka's city. There also my strength was tried in lifting Shiva's bow. Then came the responsibility of the marriage with Sita. I paid a very heavy price for marrying her. On our way back, I had to fight with Parashurama, wielding the bow of Vishnu. Then a great agony followed by the decision of our father to coronate me which ended with our exile, and you and Sita followed me all the way from Ayodhya to the forest. The sad demise of my father and the sad plight of the people of Ayodhya, who met me at Chitrakuta along with Bharata, made us leave Chitrakuta and come to Panchavati. We thought our days of sorrow had ended but they are only beginning. O Lakshmana, I suffered all the agonies because of your obedience to me and love for Sita. Today, your disobedience brought me this disaster. Otherwise, Sita would not have been carried away by vultures or demons. Lakshmana, I suspect that Sita might have been eaten by the terrible demons. Maybe at this time they are drinking her blood. She is gone. Gone forever. O Lakshmana, she is not going to return. This breaks my heart. I will not be a man again. My mind has gone with Sita. Lakshmana, I am gone."

Lamenting thus, Sri Rama sank again on the earth like an elephant stuck in the mire. Lakshmana sprinkled water on Rama's face and kneaded his feet. He spoke words of courage and consolation, saying, "Sri Rama, you are God in virtue and in strength. I know no one is equal to you in beauty, in prowess, and wisdom. Why should you worry like an ordinary man? Sita should be somewhere where we can search for her. We can walk near Godavari River and in this forest, and some clue of her whereabouts could certainly be found. O Raghurama, nothing is impossible for you. You are showing a drama for the future world to realize the depth of true affection. Let us go in search of Sita." These words of Lakshmana encouraged Rama for a while, but pained again with pangs of separation, he wailed at the loss of Sita.

"Lakshmana, this rock reminds me of Sita," said Rama. "We used to sit on that rock observing the waves of Godavari River. Today, the rock alone stands here without Sita. The river and nature were beautiful because of my love for Sita. Now my beloved is no more here. All this is meaningless to me. Lakshmana, is it day or night now? If it were night, I should have received the soothing rays of the moon. If it were day, the forest should have been bright. Perhaps the sun is afraid of me, that I may ask him to bear witness to Sita's disappearance. If it were night, how is it that the rays of the moon are scorching as if they were of the sun? Lakshmana, when difficulties come, they come one after another. I think nature is against me. Please tell me whether this is day or night." Lakshmana said, "My Lord, sun is set. It is night. Look above. The moon is smiling on you."

Sri Rama looked above and cried with agony. "O Sita, O Vaidehi, you are hiding there in the sky. Definitely it is your moon-like face which is looking at me from that distance. Sita, don't you know that my life is ebbing away without you? Come to me, my beloved, and make my forest life worth living. Where are your prayers and meditations? Where are your smiles and timely advice? O Sita, embodiment of divine virtues, there is no woman like you on earth or in heaven. Please come to the earth."

Saying thus, Rama again fainted. Lakshmana tried to console his brother, saying, "Kodandarama, if you wield your bow, the fourteen worlds will tremble. All *devas* obey your order. You are the Supreme Reality. Veiling yourself with *Maya*, O Brahman, you are showing your *lila*." Sri Rama suddenly got up and asked Lakshmana, "O Saumitri, are you exaggerating? Am I really God? If I am God, then why am I crying like a man? Why am I pained at separation from Sita? You said that at my wielding and twanging Kodanda bow, the fourteen worlds will be alarmed. I would like to do that. Let all the *lokas* know my agony so they may bring me the news of Sita. They must." Saying thus, Sri Rama pulled the strings of his Kodanda bow and fixed a sharp shaft and pointed it to the sky. The earth rocked like a cradle. The shell of the Cosmic Egg cracked. The eight guardian elephants vomited blood. The eternal tortoise that was holding the earth, perspired. The untimely cataclysm was about to happen. Brahma the creator ran to Shiva the destroyer and alarmed him that Rama, who was Vishnu, who was requested to protect *dharma* by destroying the demons, had taken the decision of destroying the whole universe. Thereupon, Shiva, Brahma and all the *devas*, hailed Sri Rama.

They offered their adorations to Sri Rama thus: "O *avatar* of Sri Vishnu, salutations unto thee. You are creator, preserver, and destroyer of the whole cosmos. You are one without a second, taking different forms. You create, protect, and destroy everything. Now for your *lila* you have taken this transcendental, human form. Goddess Lakshmi is inseparable from you. Again, for the sake of maintaining true love on earth, to teach *dharma* to the householders, you are showing this drama, as if Sita is separated from you. Hey Narayana, Sri Rama, protect the earth and protect everybody by your benevolent grace. Salutations." Hearing this prayer of the *devas*, Sri Rama assumed his human form again by untwanging the bow and placing the arrow back in the quiver. "Lakshmana, where am I? What am I doing? Why are you standing away there with fear? What happened?" Lakshmana said, "Hey Prabho, the moment you twanged the bow, you looked different. I saw you having faces on all sides, feet on all sides, and arms on all sides. The entire universe was enveloped by you, above, below, everywhere. I saw the *devas* headed by Brahma and Shiva, glorifying you. Hey Rama, you are the Infinite Truth. Now again you have assumed your human form. Let us walk."

Sri Rama began acting once again as if Sita was separated from him. "Lakshmana, look here. I see the footprints of Sita. A little away from here I see the footprints of a demon and that part of the earth is lifted as if, which shows that some terrible demon has taken Sita away from us. We must search in this direction."

As they were walking, they heard the cry of a bird echoing forth. When Rama approached him, the bird slowly opened its eyes and spoke to Rama, saying, "Sri Rama, I am Jatayu. Your beloved Sita was carried away by demon Ravana of Lanka. While he was abducting and carrying away Mother Sita, I heard her cry and flew across the sky to release her from the cruel demon. I gave a gallant battle and air fight and I would have been successful but for the deception of the demon. Being asked by him to show the spot where my life energy was, I spoke the truth by telling that it was in my wings; whereas, he showed his toe to be the abode of his *prana*. As I attacked him there on his toes, the wretched demon cut off my wings and I fell from the sky here on earth. It is by the blessings of Sita that I am alive until now, for she blessed me, saying that I will die only after your *darshan*, O Rama. The words of that Great Mother came true and I have your *darshan*. O benevolent Lord, bless me with true devotion to your lotus feet. Let me forever remain at your feet in the Kingdom of Heaven. May you give *darshan* to many devotees who are waiting for your *darshan*." Saying thus, that immortal eagle, Jatayu, touched the feet of Rama. A light emerged from the body of that bird and it merged in the feet of Rama. Sri Rama and Lakshmana cried bitterly at the loss of that great friend. Rama himself set fire to the funeral pyre of Jatayu. He blessed his soul, saying, "O noble soul of Jatayu, may you rest in peace in the Kingdom of Heaven. You are a true devotee and a friend, for you have sacrificed your life for the sake of your Master. May your example inspire many that the way of spirituality is only for those who sacrifice themselves at the altar of the Lord."

Story of Kabandha

Rama and Lakshmana proceeded further in search of Sita. Again their left eye and left shoulders throbbed. Rama said, "O Lakshmana, our misery is not yet over. Something dangerous is ahead. Let us gather our strength and rely on ourselves. May the true love of Sita protect us."

Within a few moments, they heard a loud clamor that made their blood run cold. They saw a hideous looking demon stretching his arms to nearly four miles distance and devouring elephants, lions, tigers, and herds of deer. Whatever was available, those long arms could reach it and that demon, Kabandha, snatching the animals by his hand, would swallow them. The demon had no head. He had but one eye in his chest and the belly had a cave-like mouth. Such a hideous creature they had never seen before. He tried to snatch Rama and Lakshmana to crush them out of existence. Rama and Lakshmana cut off his two arms with their sharp swords and shattered his body by their shafts. To their amazement, they saw a celestial person emerging out of that demon body. He said that he was a *gandharva*, a celestial musician, the son of Danu. He once insulted a great master named Sthulashira by taking a huge shape and incurred the anger of the sage. The sage cursed him to take birth as a monster, whose body should be barrel-shaped. Accordingly, he was born that way, "Hey Rama," the celestial person said, "by your *darshan*, I am released from this terrible demon body. Rama, as you go further in this direction, you are going to meet a great devotee named Shabari. She is going to tell you what happened to Sita; please bless her with your *darshan*." Saying thus, that celestial person ascended to heaven.

Shabari

Shabari was a hunter's daughter. The night before her marriage, she saw thousands of goats and sheep being brought by her father. When she asked the reason for bringing so many animals, he said he was going to kill all the goats and sheep for her marriage dinner. Her heart moved with compassion, and during the early hours of the morning, she renounced the world and ran away to meet a Master. She met, after days of traveling, a Master named Sage Matanga at the foot of Mountain Rishyamuka. There she lived with her *guru* serving him with all devotion. When her *guru*, Matanga, was about to depart from the body, Shabari said, "O Master, I served you throughout my life. I want to reach the same abode of peace which you will reach." Thereupon, Sage Matanga said, "Shabari, you dedicated your whole life in search of Truth. I am not fortunate enough to see Rama face to face, but by the virtue of your true *seva* (service) to me, Rama shall certainly give you *darshan*; therefore, wait until he comes." Saying thus, Sage Matanga, sitting in lotus posture, withdrew his *prana* and *apana* and took them both, along with the soul, up through the spine and left his body by breaking open the tenth aperture, merging in God.

As per her *guru's* words, she waited for the arrival of Rama. Now the news came to her that Rama might come at any time. Blind due to her old age, she didn't know what to do. She was overwhelmed with joy that Rama was coming, so she went out of her *ashram* with the help of a walking stick to pluck some berry fruits. She would pluck a fruit, first taste it, and if it was sweet she would put it in her basket, and if it was bitter she would throw it. She just wanted to give the good and sweet fruits to her God. The thought never came to her mind that she should not taste it before it was offered. In *bhakti*, or love, faults are not seen by God.

As she was plucking the fruit, even a small breeze would make her feel that Rama had come and suddenly she would call, "Rama." When there would be no response, she would continue plucking the fruits. Thinking of Rama's transcendental form, she would enter into meditation. As she was plucking the fruit, she was mentally offering the flowers and fruits to Rama. Thus, collecting a few fruits, Shabari went back to her humble hut.

At times she would feel so exalted that she would burst into laughter, thinking her greatest desire was fulfilled, and then suddenly she would feel depressed thinking that such a great Lord might not visit her humble hut. Then she remembered the words of her *guru* and felt glad at heart that Rama will certainly come because he is God and God always cares for his devotees.

Even though hundreds of other *yogis* were waiting to receive Rama in their *ashrams*, Rama went only to Shabari's *ashram* because of her sincere devotion. The Lord announced himself at the door of her humble hut, saying, "Shabari! Rama and Lakshmana, the sons of Dasharatha, are here." Shabari was beside herself with joy. She entered into different *bhavas* or ecstatic states of consciousness. Horripilation, perspiration, tears of joy, words getting choked in her throat, stupefaction, pangs of separation, at times loud laughter, at other times crying loudly, with uplifted arms, dancing and singing the Holy Name, these were some of the *bhavas* which she experienced. Finally, she fell at the feet of Rama, bathing them with her tears. With joined palms, that noble devotee of Rama prayed thus, "Hey Rama, how compassionate you are. Among innumerable creatures you have created, I am the humble one. There were so many exalted *yogis* waiting for your *darshan*, but you came to this unworthy devotee of yours. This clearly shows that you will neither see whether a devotee lives in a palace or humble hut, whether he is erudite or ignorant. You will neither see caste nor color. You will only see the true *bhakti* or devotion; but my Lord, I still do not know whether my devotion has pleased you or not. I do not have anything to offer other than my heart, but here are some berry fruits. May it please you, my Lord, to partake them."

So saying, Shabari offered the fruits to Raghava. When Sri Rama was tasting them, Lakshmana said, "O brother, it seems Shabari has tasted them already; therefore, they are unworthy of eating." Rama said, "Lakshmana, you know how many types of food I have tasted but I tell you the truth, nothing could equal these berry fruits, offered with such devotion by Shabari. You taste them, then alone you will know. Whosoever offers a fruit or a leaf, flower or water with love, I partake it with great joy." Lakshmana also had a great experience tasting the fruit. Pleased with her devotion, Sri Rama asked Shabari, saying, "Shabari, you are my true devotee. Ask any boon of your choice." Shabari said, "Sri Rama, celestials and sages meditate for thousands of years for your *darshan*. Today you are here in this transcendental form. Would it be possible for me to have the *darshan* of your physical form, even though you have revealed your form to me in my heart?" Sri Rama blessed her with eyesight to have his *darshan*. Shabari saw that glorious, supraphysical form which contained the essence of the whole universe. Gazing at Rama's incomparable beauty, Shabari enjoyed ineffable peace. She saw the Lord of the Universe sitting there with knotted locks, Rudrakshi beads, bark garments, bow and arrows, a divine smile dancing on his nectarian face, and a soothing grace issuing forth from his lustrous eyes. Shabari saluted the Lord again and again and prayed for *bhakti* and *mukti*.

Sri Ramachandra made her sit comfortably and spoke to her very lovingly. "Shabari, do you have any questions?" Shabari said, "My Lord, you are the answer to all my questions, but, as you are giving me this opportunity to ask you, I have one question. Among many types of spiritual disciplines, what pleases you most and how can you be easily attained? Rama, I ask this question for all your devotees." Sri Rama spoke, "Shabari, nothing pleases me as pure devotion. Such pure devotion is expressed in nine ways, known as *nava-vidha bhakti* or nine-fold devotion. First is *satsang* or association with love-intoxicated devotees. The second is to develop a deep taste for hearing my nectarian stories. The third is service to the *guru* who inspires everyone with divine love. Fourth is to sing my *kirtana* unabashed. *Japa* or repetition of my Holy Name and chanting my *bhajans* are the fifth expressions of my *bhakti*. To follow the scriptural injunctions always and to practice control of senses, noble character, and selfless service, these are the expressions in the sixth mode of *bhakti*. Seeing me everywhere manifested in this world and worshipping my saints more than myself is the seventh stage of this love. To find no fault with anyone and to be contented with one's lot is the eighth mode of *bhakti*. Unreserved surrender, with total faith in my strength, is the ninth and the highest stage of love. Shabari, anyone who practices one of these nine modes of my *bhakti* pleases me most and reaches me without fail. That which is most difficult for the greatest *yogis* was easily attained by you, Shabari, because of your sincere devotion. This is the testimony of my *bhakti*." Saying thus, Sri Rama blessed Shabari with pure *bhakti*. Rama said, "Shabari, would you kindly show me the way which leads to Lake Pampa? Also, do you know of Sita's abduction?" Shabari said, "Rama, if you go this way, you will reach Lake Pampa.

Very near to that is Rishyamuka Mountain. Sugriva and his friends live on that mountain and will certainly serve you in searching Sita."

Saying thus, she prepared her funeral pyre and, meditating on Rama, happily plunged into the fire. Sri Rama blessed her with his Kingdom of Heaven or *mukti*. Three worlds glorified Shabari's *bhakti*!

Pampa

Rama and Lakshmana walked the way toward Pampa. The forest and the atmosphere near Lake Pampa were simply beautiful. Seeing the limpid waters of Lake Pampa, Sri Rama bathed in it with Lakshmana. He saw the beautifully blossomed lotuses there and remembered the lotus-like face of Sita. Feeling pangs of separation, Sri Rama once again cried bitterly and told Lakshmana, "O my brother, days and months have passed. We have not yet been able to find Sita's whereabouts. My life is worthless without that embodiment of chastity." Lakshmana consoled his brother and both of them said their prayers and began walking. The indescribable beauty of the trees and the flowers made Rama forget his grief. The cool breeze brought the fragrance of the blossomed flowers, giving both of them great happiness. Like two lions, Rama and Lakshmana wandered in that forest garden, wondering at the beauty of nature.

Here ends the third book entitled *Aranya Kanda*, or the forest canto.

BOOK IV

KISHKINDA KANDA

In the case of a great *avatar* of God, many *devas* and angels incarnate ahead to pave the way and to serve the Lord. Such an *avatar* is known as *Lila Avatar*. When Lord Vishnu decided to take His incarnation on earth at the request of *devas* for the destruction of Ravana and Kumbhakarna, Brahma, the creator, told all the *devas* to take incarnation to prepare the minds of the people and the platform for the coming one.

Ravana, the ten-headed demon, had a boon from Creator Brahma, as per his wish, that he would not meet death by any of the celestials or gods, but he would meet death only by men and monkeys. When Ravana prayed for his boon, he thought that he could easily vanquish or kill men and monkeys. That is the reason why God incarnated as Rama the man, and all the part manifestations of God became the monkeys.

To pave the way for the Lord, millions of *devas*, through their part manifestation, were born as monkeys. For example, the part manifestation of Brahma the creator became Jambavan; of the wind god, Hanuman; of fire, Neela; of Indra the head of the angels, Vali; of the sun god, Sugriva; of the twin celestial physicians known as Ashwini *devatas*, the two great monkeys known as Mainda and Dvivida; of the divine sculptor Vishwakarma, Nala, and so on. Thus, nearly seventy-two million part manifestations of God were born as monkeys. They were not ordinary monkeys. They were very tall, bright-bodied, and very strong. They were conversing in Sanskrit language and were great devotees of God. If this is the epic description, historically speaking they were strong-bodied men with monkey banners.

Esoterically, Hanuman is *prana*, or cosmic life and the life in human body, and seventy-two million monkeys are the vibrations both in the individual and the universe. Rama is the Self. So the life principle is always the servant of the Self and the life vibrates through seventy-two thousand *nadis* (astral tubes) in the body and through seventy-two million ways in the cosmos. An epic could be interpreted in millions of ways as according to the context, but the great masters think it is beautiful to see Rama, the God-man, moving among birds, animals, and monkeys, making friendship with the whole universe. For our story purpose, it is beautiful to know that the monkeys participated in a God-man's work in restoring *dharma*. In all world religion scriptures, the supra-mental principles are always explained through the bodies or faces of the beasts.

To return to the story, Sugriva, the son of the sun god, saw from his high mountain the two strong-bodied men walking on the shore of Lake Pampa. As he was driven to that mountain by his elder brother, Vali, he was afraid that Vali might have sent those two strong men to capture and destroy him. Doubting thus, Sugriva called all his monkey chieftains and discussed the situation with them for a while. He knew, among all the monkey chieftains, Hanuman was the one who could take any form he liked and could read the minds of the people and understand their thoughts without revealing his secret; therefore, Sugriva requested Hanuman to go immediately to those wandering men on the shore of Pampa to find out who they were and why they were wandering there. Accordingly, Hanuman disguised himself as a hermit, and within moments reached the shores of Pampa. Even though he wanted to maintain his secret, no sooner his eyes fell on the face of Rama, something wonderful happened to Hanuman. From toe to head there was a cosmic electricity moving in his body and he felt like crying with joy for no reason. He felt like falling at the feet of that sky-colored Rama. However he tried, he could not contain his feelings. As he was disguised in the form of a *brahmin* hermit, he should have chanted the *mantras* of blessing to warriors Rama and Lakshmana; instead, automatically his palms were joined in front of Rama and his head was bent spontaneously. Hanuman knew from the holy scripture that if, on meeting a person without introduction, even for a moment, you feel a peace which you have never enjoyed before, and if your hair stands on end and palms join with head bent, then the one you are meeting should be considered your *guru*. Hanuman thought that he had met his Master. Out of deep devotion, Hanuman questioned, saying, "O strong-bodied, beautiful men, who are you? It is impossible for me to think that you are human beings. You definitely should be either Vishnu and Shiva walking over the earth or some twin angels appearing in blue and white bodies. Even though you are hiding your regal dignity with knotted locks and bark robes, the compassion, love, integrity, and the power which is emerging from you makes me feel that you are definitely disguised divine beings. What caused you to walk in this forest place? The sharp-pointed grass and stones here, compared to the blossomed red, lotus-like soles of your feet, bring pain to me when you walk over this hazardous path. I am very eager to know from your mouth your story."

Whosoever is soft-spoken, dignified, speaks with reverence, and is disciplined, obedient, and eager to know the truth, should be considered a disciple. Such is the commandment of the scriptures. So just as Hanuman felt in Rama, his Master, similarly, Rama felt in Hanuman, his disciple. Turning toward Lakshmana, Rama said, "O son of Sumitra, I have never heard anyone until now speak so softly the perfect Sanskrit language properly intoned with rhyme and rhythm. When this hermit speaks, there is no slip of the tongue, not a single mistake; it is neither harsh, nor high-toned or low-toned; it is just beautiful. He is so precise; speaks only to the point and to the context. He is most cultured; his speech is so resonant and filled with friendly vibrations. I do not think he is a hermit or a *brahmin*. If it were so, he should have chanted the *mantras* of blessing to us. Instead, he saluted us. Lakshmana, I am sure he is well-trained in *Rig Veda*. I have no doubt that he has memorized *Yajur Veda*, too. When he speaks, it is celestial music. Therefore, I think he must be a singer of *Sama Veda* and a master of *Atharva Veda*. I am so fascinated with this man. All my sorrow at the separation of Sita, at least for the time being, has left me."

Turning to Hanuman, Rama said, "O hermit, I am Rama, the son of Dasharatha. This is my younger brother, Lakshmana, the son of Sumitra. To fulfill the words of promise of my father to my step-mother, Kaikeyi, I have been exiled to the forest. Along with me, my wife Sita and this brother Lakshmana came to the forest, but unfortunately, my wife Sita was carried away by some demon. We were searching for Sita and in that search we have come here."

No sooner Hanuman heard that he was Rama than he entered into trance-like state. His hair stood on end and tears of joy stained his cheeks, for he had heard from the lips of his mother, as a child, about the glory of Rama. She virtually initiated him in *Taraka Mantra* or the Holy Name of Rama. She insisted that Hanuman chant and meditate on Rama until Rama gives him *darshan*. His mother had advised him that once he meets Rama, he should dedicate his whole life to the service of the great Master and manifest to the world the glory of service to

God. Remembering all this, Hanuman again and again entered into *bhaya* and circumambulated Rama and Lakshmana chanting His Holy Name. "Rama, Kodandarama, Pattabhirama, Sitarama, namo, namo. Salutations to you, Rama, the wielder of Kodanda, kindly accept me as your *dasa.* My mother has told me about you, O incarnation of Vishnu. You have incarnated in this human form for the protection of the world. I will offer my body, mind, strength, and life for your *seva.* I am the friend and the minister to Sugriva. Sugriva dwells in the nearby mountain called Rishyamuka. I can carry you there, my Lord, and introduce you to Sugriva. I am sure that you will alleviate his grief and he will be an immense help in searching for Mother Sita."

Sri Rama was wonderstruck at the single-minded devotion of the hermit. Rama questioned him, "May I know who are you? Who are your parents and what is your name?" Hanuman replied, "Sri Rama, my father is Vayu, the wind god; my mother is Anjanidevi. They call me Hanuman." "What?" Rama exclaimed. "Are you Hanuman? I have heard so much about you but what I have heard was about a Hanuman who is as tall as a palm tree, whose body is shining like a diamond. But you are a hermit. How should I know that you are that Hanuman?" With great devotion, Hanuman said, "O my Master, nothing is unknown to you. If it is your will, I will reveal my true body." Saying thus, Hanuman chanted "Raghuramachandra Maharaj Ki Jai," and revealed his true form. The mountainous body of the son of wind god eclipsed thousands of suns and moons. Rama and Lakshmana were wonderstruck and were overjoyed. Bending before the two great brothers, Hanuman said, "My Lord, this body of mine is your chariot. Please sit on my shoulder. Lakshmana, you sit on my other shoulder and both of you bless me to serve you forever." Accordingly, Rama and Lakshmana sat on his shoulders. Within the twinkling of an eye, the immortal Hanuman took them to the top peak of the Rishyamuka Mountain. There he introduced Rama and Lakshmana to Sugriva, his chief. Hanuman brought all monkeys together and worshipped Rama and Lakshmana. Washing his feet and offering water to his hands, he sang in praise of Rama. Collecting the fuel, he organized a campfire and made Sugriva and Rama accept one another as great friends making the fire god the witness to their friendship.

Sugriva narrated a sad story to Sri Ramachandra. He said, "Rama, my elder brother Vali has wronged me and has driven me away, depriving me of all enjoyments. Vali is very powerful and strong. Early every morning he flies to four oceans, bathes and pours oblations and returns to his kingdom of Kishkinda. Despite his meditations and knowledge, he is not humble. He is a terror even to the demons. Once the ten-headed demon Ravana went to fight with him. At that time he was bathing in the ocean. Then Ravana went from behind to surprise him. Vali just wrapped him by his tail, dipped him into the ocean and made him hang to the cradle of his son, Angada, as a toy. After some time they released him and sent him back to Lanka. At another time, a demon called Mayavi came to fight with him. They fought, throwing stones and rocks over one another until finally demon Mayavi ran into a cave. Vali wanted to destroy him so he asked me to follow him to the cave and both of them went into the cave. Vali made me stand at the gate of the cave and asked me to stay there until he returned. He chased Mayavi in the cave, but for a number of months Vali never came out. I waited and waited until finally I saw a stream of blood issuing forth from the cave. This made me feel that my brother Vali might have been killed by the demon and I had every fear that he might kill me and our subjects as well. Out of fear, I closed the opening of the cave with a huge mountain so that Mayavi should never come out. After that, I returned to the palace and proclaimed myself as the king of Kishkinda and ruled over the subjects righteously. It seemed my elder brother Vali came near the opening of the cave after killing the demon and found it closed by a mountain. He kicked the mountain out of the way and rushed to the kingdom with great anger toward me. He suspected I wanted to get rid of him and he thought that was why I placed the mountain at the gate of the cave. He had no patience to listen to me. He just drove me out of Kishkinda, depriving me of all wealth and enjoyments. He forcibly kept my wife in prison and chased me from place to place. Wandering here and there, finally I came and settled in this mountain of Rishyamuka where he cannot come due to a curse uttered by Sage Matanga."

Sri Rama asked the cause of the curse to Vali by Matanga. Sugriva resumed, "Rama, there came one day a demon named Dundubhi in the form of a mountainous bull. He began attacking everybody and calling everyone to fight with him. He killed many and dashed the rocks to pieces, demonstrating his prowess. When my brother Vali was invited by him to fight, he fought with him gallantly. It was like two mountains chasing one another and fighting with one another. Finally, Vali pounded him to death. After that, he kicked the mountainous bull-body of the demon Dundubhi and it fell four miles away in the *ashram* of Sage Matanga. Seeing the *ashram* atmosphere polluted by the carcass of the bull demon, the enraged sage hurled a curse as a thunderbolt on the head of my brother Vali, saying, "Whoever caused this pollution by throwing the demon's dead body here, suffers the punishment of death if he enters this Rishyamuka mountain *ashram*." Sugriva said, "Sri Rama, due to this curse of the sage, my elder brother Vali is afraid to come to this mountain. Even though the sage has died long ago, the curse remains on Vali forever. Finding this place safer than any other, I have settled here on this mountain with Hanuman and other monkey chieftains. Sri Rama, my wife is undergoing various chastisements by Vali. Vali thinks might is right and is very arrogant. I understand from Hanuman that you have been deprived of your wife Sita, as the ten-headed demon Ravana has carried her away. Sri Rama, I would like to show you some very valuable information about this.

"One day as we were sitting and discussing something on this mountain, we heard a cry from a woman flying in an aerial car. She was loudly chanting, "Rama, Rama." She tore away the end of her *sari*, placed some of her ornaments, tied them, and hurled them over the mountain where we were sitting. I have kept them very safe. If you like, I will show them to you." Sri Rama was very eager to see them, whereupon Sugriva brought and handed them to Rama. Sri Rama untied them and saw the different ornaments of Sita given to her by Sage Atri's wife, Anasuya. Melting in tears, Rama explained to Lakshmana the different ornaments, but Lakshmana did not recognize them. Finally, when Rama showed her toe-rings, Lakshmana said, "Rama, I could neither recognize the earrings nor necklaces, but this toe-ring of Sita's I definitely know because I used to prostrate every day to her lotus-like feet." Hearing these words of Lakshmana, Sri Rama and all *vaanaras* shed profuse tears, feeling the sincerity and purity of Lakshmana. Even though he lived with Rama and Sita all these years, he never looked at Sita's body or ornaments intentionally and therefore, he couldn't recognize any of her ornaments other than the toe-ring. Such was the sincerity of Lakshmana!

Now Rama knew for certain that Sita was taken by the demon Ravana of Lanka. He entered into a covenant with Sugriva that he will restore Sugriva's kingdom and wife by killing Vali and in return, Sugriva pledged that he will search for Sita and find out her whereabouts with the help of all the *vaanaras*. Sugriva said, "Rama, I believe in your strength, even though I have never seen any demonstration of your prowess, but I have told you that

Vali kicked the body of Dundubhi four miles away. If you could be kind enough to demonstrate your strength, that may bring a great confidence to my heart."

Hearing these words of Sugriva, Sri Rama twanged his Kodanda bow. The whole universe trembled. When he hit one arrow, the seven mighty trees that had their roots in the nether regions were toppled down, and the arrow went to an island, killed many demons, and returned to Rama's quiver. Seeing this, Sugriva perspired. Then Rama saw the huge carcass of demon Dundubhi lying there even after so many years. No sooner he kicked the carcass than it was thrown hundreds of miles away. Sugriva fell prostrate at the feet of Rama, craving forgiveness for his ignorance. Now he was convinced of the strength of Rama. Rama asked Sugriva to invite Vali to fight. Rama assured him that he would stand behind him and slay Vali.

Sugriva, filled with the inspiration of Rama, went and roared at the gate of Vali's palace, inviting him to fight with him. Vali was very much upset with Sugriva's attitude and wanted him to be crushed out of existence. Both brothers looked alike in every limb of their body. Their faces being alike, it was very difficult for observers to find out who was who. The surrounding rocks and mountains were finished as they hurled them over one another and fought severely. Finally, the strong Vali was able to break the hipbone of Sugriva by kicking him and Sugriva fell unconscious, writhing with pain. When he gathered his senses, Vali warned him, saying, "O Sugriva, this time I forgive you and let you go, as you are my brother. If you show your face once again, I shall crush you out of existence." Saying thus, Vali went back to his palace puffed up with arrogance. Suffering great pain, Sugriva slowly approached Rama and said, "Rama, *namaskar*. No more friendship with you. I realize now, God and *guru* are to be worshipped from a distance. I believed in you and you deceived me. Vali would have sent me to the abode of death but for his mercy toward me as his brother. Rama, I should have realized that you are not God but just an ordinary man. I should have known that a man who cannot protect his wife from the ten-headed demon, how can he restore my wife from the strong Vali? Rama, I am done away with you. Salutations."

Sri Rama tried to console him by saying, "O Sugriva, please do not misunderstand. I could have killed Vali easily, but both of you look so alike that I was afraid that my arrow may hit you instead of Vali. Lakshmana, bring that beautiful garland made of the flower Gaja-pushpika. Let me adorn the neck of Sugriva with that garland and let him call Vali immediately to fight with him again so that I may slay the arrogant Vali and restore his wife to him." Saying thus, Sri Rama put the garland around the neck of Sugriva and asked him to once again call Vali to fight with him.

It was not easy for Sugriva to believe Rama so quickly because the strong kick of Vali had disjointed his hipbone, so he doubted Rama's valor and promise. Somehow Hanuman restored his faith and healed his hipbone, inspiring him to invite Vali to fight with him. Sugriva roared again at the gate of the palace, saying, "O Vali, O Vali, come again to fight with me." Vali, who had just returned to his palace, flew into a rage hearing the roar of Sugriva. He decided to pound him to pieces in this fight. Drinking wine, with bloodshot eyes, as Vali was proceeding toward the gate, he was stopped by his chaste wife Tara. She said, "My lord, evil portents are visible. Jackals are crying. My right eye is throbbing. This time, some danger awaits you. Our beloved son Angada has brought the message to me that Lord Vishnu's incarnation, Rama, is backing Sugriva. It seems he has inspired Sugriva's calling you so soon to fight him. I believe Rama is God who has come to restore *dharma*, so I implore you not to go to fight with Sugriva as you might meet with the pain of death."

Vali set aside her remarks by saying, "Tara, don't you know how powerful I am? Don't you remember that the very same ten-headed demon, Ravana, who has stolen the wife of this Rama, was wrapped in my tail and hung to the cradle of our son Angada as a toy. As this Rama could not protect his wife from the demon, how can he restore the wife of Sugriva who is imprisoned by me? Therefore, worry not about this Rama. I shall send all these people to the abode of death." Saying thus, the arrogant Vali went out to fight with Sugriva. Vali gave a very severe battle. Squeezing Sugriva under his arms, he decided to put an end to his life and Sugriva, with his pale eyes, looked at Rama for protection. Rama, who was hiding behind a tree, struck Vali's bosom with his very powerful arrow. That fire-emitting arrow pierced the bosom of Vali and came out his back. However he tried to pull the arrow out, he could not do so, as Rama's arrow never returns until it finishes the person at whom it is hurled. The arrow was pulling his intestines out and the strong-bodied Vali, vomiting blood, fell on the ground unconscious for some time. Whirling his body round and round and turning his eyeballs on all sides, the great Vali looked like the setting sun. He cried out loudly, saying, "Where is that man who hit the arrow at me deceivingly? If he has come to restore *dharma*, let him come and answer my question; otherwise, I shall not have peace at death."

As Vali challenged thus, Avatar Rama walked toward Vali with majestic steps and sat near him with his Kodanda bow and Lakshmana by his side. Gazing at the transcendental beauty of Rama, Vali felt great peace but as he was confused, he challenged Rama about the intricacies of *dharma*. He said, "Are you that Rama, the so-called incarnation of Vishnu? Tell me how many years you have practiced killing innocent ones standing behind trees. You look like a hunter who is expert in killing animals from behind. I cannot call you an *avatar*. If you should be so clever in killing from behind, how much more clever should be your *guru* who taught you this form of fighting. Ahhh Rama, you are a wonderful *avatar*.

"Ohhh, I know, aren't you the same Rama who is the son of Dasharatha of Solar race? I can understand why you hit me from behind. Seeing that you are unworthy of your throne, you were kicked out of your kingdom by your stepmother and exiling yourself in the forest, you had no food or shelter and you allowed some demon to carry away your wife. It is no wonder you hit me from behind because I think you should be very hungry. According to the scriptural injunctions, a king or a hunter can kill an animal from behind, only for the sake of flesh. But did you forget, Rama, that monkey flesh is forbidden by the scriptures? Out of your hunger you might have forgotten all scriptural injunctions. If that were so, I pity you. Come on. As you have killed me, peel my skin, drink my blood, eat my flesh, and be happy.

"Rama, I have never attacked Ayodhya. Nor have I carried away any women from Ayodhya nor I have assaulted any queens of your city. Not even in a dream have I done any wrong to you or your forefathers. What right do you have to interfere in our affair and to hit me from behind? If you are born to restore *dharma*, tell me the secret of *dharma* which empowered you to kill me.

"Rama, what a deceptive figure you are. Ahh, your matted locks, your bark robes, smearing holy ashes all over the body, decked with Rudrakshi beads, you really look like a great *yogi*, but Rama, in your heart you are so cruel and you have no compassion for animals like me. How dare you call yourself Vishnu's *avatar*.

"Rama, even though you think that I enjoyed my younger brother's wife by imprisoning her in my palace or deprived my brother of our kingdom, how can you, an exile, interfere in our affair? By your human standards, these things may look ridiculous and sinful but not for us, who are animals; therefore, all that you have tried to do is just an ignorant game. Think, and you will know whether you have observed *dharma*.

"Ohhh, Rama, who named you, who named you as Rama? That sweet name brings a transcendental peace to my agonized soul at the time of death but you are unworthy of that name. Please remove that name from your person for that should be the name of God.

"Rama, this *vaijayanti* garland was presented to me by my father Indra with a boon that whosoever fights with me, half of his strength will be automatically squeezed by the power of the garland. That is why you hid behind the tree; otherwise, in a righteous war, I would have just pulled your bow and arrow with my hand and snapped them into two, but now it is too late. You have done the most heinous crime. Before I die, give me the right answer according to the scriptures: What is it that sanctioned you to kill me?

"Rama, if you had even hinted that the ten-headed Ravana had stolen away your wife, there would have been no necessity for your suffering. Even as a fisherman pulls the fish out by the fishing rod, similarly, I would have sent my tail to Lanka and pulled the demon out from his throne and would have made him surrender your beloved Sita. For long ago I wrapped him in my tail, which I hope he has not forgotten. Now what is the use of talking? You are unfortunate.

"Rama, what a friendship you made with my beggarly brother. You have lost your wife, and he his wife. Naturally, therefore, you have become friends without having any strength to restore one another's wives. Killing me, restoring Sugriva's wife, gathering all the *vaanaras* together, sending them in all directions, searching for Sita, bridging the ocean, going to Lanka, killing all the demons, and afterward bringing Sita back. Ohh, this would need as much effort as your ancestor Bhagiratha, who went to bring the Ganges to the earth.

Forget about it. Give me the right explanation for the wrong which you have done to me."

Sri Rama, Lakshmana, and thousands of monkey chieftains heard the challenging speech of Vali and were astonished. Celestials and angels, sages and saints, gathered from all directions to hear the answer from Rama's mouth. Like the rumbling of a cloud, with a deep voice, tuning himself to his Divine Self, Rama spoke the Truth. "Hear O valiant Vali. I am Rama, the incarnation of Vishnu, and have come in this human form for the restoration of *dharma. Devas* and angels, sages and saints, and Hanuman know this fact. Perfect as I am in my thought, word, and deed, I have done only that which is *dharma.* With your imperfect mind, you cannot envision the truth that I speak, but I will try to convince you.

"Using the words of promise of my father as an excuse, I exiled myself to the forest purposely, taking Sita and Lakshmana with me for the continuance of the *lila* which I wanted to manifest. I exiled myself so that hundreds of *yogis* who were waiting for my *darshan*, may get it and those to whom I have to give *mukti* should be given that. You are one among them, having practiced the spiritual discipline of morning meditations by bathing and pouring oblations in four oceans everyday. If you were a devotee, you would have been given the same *mukti* in a soothing way. Arrogant as you are, despite the knowledge which you have, you were given this punishment so that your soul need not suffer rebirth once again. Having been killed by me and uttering my name at the time of death, and seeing my divine form with your eyes, you will have no more *karma* left with you for attaining the final beatitude.

"If kings like you do not show the ideal to the subjects and humanity, all will not follow the standard that is set by an ideal man. Knowingly you have wronged your brother and knowingly you have wronged his wife. Now tell me. According to the scripture, a daughter, sister-in-law, and daughter-in-law, are to be treated equally as one's own daughter. Imprisoning your sister-in-law, you have enjoyed her wrongly and have made your brother suffer endlessly, thinking that might is right. According to the scriptures, a torture of death is the only punishment for such a crime. Vali, tell the truth in my presence. Have you performed your *dharma*? If not, you are worthy of this punishment. This alone relieves you from the sins you have done and your soul is purified now by this punishment.

"If you tell me that I should not interfere in your affair, then who else should? As the Lord of Preservation, it is my *dharma* to destroy evil; therefore, I have hit you. If, out of your ignorance, you do not agree that I am an *avatar*, then I also want to tell you, it is the kings of the Solar race who are the head of this whole earth. Being born as the eldest son of Dasharatha, even though exiled, still my sandals are ruling over Ayodhya. Look at the signet ring given to me by my father at the time of his death. This is the insignia of royalty, that after my fourteen years of exile, I am to be coronated as the king of Ayodhya. You are a petty king under my jurisdiction. I am the king disguised; therefore, I have every right to punish you.

"Vali, you are arguing with me saying that you are an animal and human law cannot be applied in your case. At the same time you are telling me that you are the son of Indra, who has given you the garland of *vaijayanti*. This shows that you are assuming a monkey body, being a part manifestation of Indra. You assumed this body as other *devatas* for the purpose of paving my way; but instead, you come in my way and therefore, as an *avatar*, I have to send you back from where you have come. See in your meditation whether what I speak is true or not at the hour of this death.

"Vali, you are continuously saying that I hit you from behind. This argument is futile. Of course I hid behind the tree but not behind you. I was behind Sugriva, who was facing you; therefore, I was facing you. If I hit you from behind, my arrow would have pierced your back and come out of your bosom; instead, you can see my arrow pierced your bosom first and then pierced your back. Also, for an ignorant man, even though God is in front, he would say that God is hiding. Remove the veil of your arrogance and see I am right in front of you and in all directions.

"Suppose you still have doubt in my personality. If you touch my feet and tell that you will share your kingdom with your brother Sugriva, I will not only forgive you but also withdraw my arrow and give you life right now. Do you wish to live?

"Finally Vali, I shall vouchsafe to you the blessings of your third eye. Through this, see my divine nature and hold your peace." Saying thus, Rama revealed his true nature to the dying Vali. A great inspiration and strength welled up in the body of Vali and by the blessings of the third eye, he saw his creator and preserver, in his true form. He raised his eyes and saw him in sky, in air, in water, in fire, and earth. He saw every atom singing his Holy Name and all the angels and archangels glorifying him. He saw Rama as the Eternal Man, Purushottama, glorified in the *Vedas*. He saw Sage Vasishta, Vishwamitra, Sharabhanga, Suteekshna, Agastya, and several sages recognizing Rama as an *avatar*. The whole story of Rama was revealed before his third eye like a drama or *lila*.

Filled with rapturous ecstasy and supreme *bhakti*, Vali joined his palms to Raghava and glorified him. "O Infinite Truth, salutations unto thee. O auspicious abode of Truth and peace, adorations unto thee. Time and again thou hast taken incarnation for the protection of humanity and the *Vedas*. You were Matsya, Kurma, Varaha, Narasimha, Vamana, Parashurama, and now you have incarnated as Sri Ramachandra. Sita is Lakshmi, and we, the celestials have assumed this form of monkeys to do your *seva* ignorantly. I spoke ill words toward you, the One who is glorified in the *Vedas* and the *Upanishads*. O compassionate Lord, I do not want to live in this sinful body which has committed so many wrongs. I feel very blessed that at the hour of my death caused by you, you have discoursed on *Sanatana Dharma* and revealed your true form unto me. I have no desire to remain living in this body. Chanting your Holy Name, let me depart from this body right now. All that I pray is complete forgiveness for all the abuses I did and all the sins I committed, knowingly or unknowingly. How could a tree stand before a tornado? How could any of my sins remain after your *darshan*? Bless me, by coming very near to me and allow me to place my head on your lotus feet and let my soul merge in you." Saying thus, Vali entered into the highest state of *bhakti*, known as *Parabhakti*. Sri Rama, who is easily attracted by such devotion, forgave him and blessed him.

Vali called his younger brother, Sugriva, and told him in front of Rama that he had no more enmity toward him and he should not feel the wrongs done by his elder brother as he has already been punished properly and forgiven by the Lord. Holding the feet of Rama, Vali said, "Sugriva, do not behave like me. When the kingdom is restored to you, as power always corrupts, serve Sri Rama, as you are privileged to do that." He called his wife Tara and his son Angada and made them both fall at the feet of Rama and said, "Rama, please take away the last attachment that I have for my wife and son. However I try, I still feel affection toward my son Angada. Please accept him as your *dasa* so that his life may be dedicated to your service and bless Tara with peace." As heavenly angels played their trumpets, Sage Narada and Tumbura sang the glory of Hari, and celestial nymphs showered flowers, Vali's soul departed from his body by breaking open the tenth aperture. Even as a drop, merging in the ocean, loses its individuality, similarly, Vali merged in the all-pervading consciousness of Rama.

After the performance of obsequies by Sugriva and Angada, Sri Rama released Sugriva's wife from the prison, restored her to Sugriva, and installed him over the throne of Kishkinda.

Sugriva said, "Rama, as the rainy season has approached, during that period all monkeys will be resting, so after the rainy season the search for Sita could begin."

Sri Rama and Lakshmana agreed to that proposal and retired to Prasravana mountain. Sugriva drowned himself in sense pleasures and completely forgot Rama's work.

In pain, man remembers God. In pleasure, he forgets God. One who remembers God in both pain and pleasure equally, attains immortality.

Suffering the pangs of separation from Sita, Sri Rama spent the rainy season with great agony. Seeing that Sugriva had not yet begun the search for Sita, Rama called Lakshmana and said, "Lakshmana, I can bear no more the pain of separation from Sita. I thought Sugriva to be a true friend and now I can see he cares not for his word of promise, only indulging in sense pleasures. Will you kindly go to Kishkinda and remind him of his duty?" Lakshmana was very angry at Sugriva for his negligence. He said, "Rama, a king sunken in ego and sense pleasures, forgetting *dharma*, should be punished with the pain of death. I am going to kill Sugriva for deceiving us. Please give me your permission." Sri Rama said, "Lakshmana, anger is the arch enemy of peace. Anger destroys right discrimination. Control your anger. Do not think of killing Sugriva. Remind him of his duty and inspire him. I am sure he will serve us."

Making obeisance to Rama, Lakshmana went to Kishkinda. Seeing the abodes of the monkey chieftains, Lakshmana came to the gate of the palace of Sugriva. Seeing Angada there, he sent word to Sugriva. Angada said to Sugriva, "O dear uncle, Lakshmana seems to be angry at me. Unless we calm him down with our promise to discharge our duty, we will be in trouble." Hanuman also insisted that Sugriva should send word to all the monkey chieftains and gather all the monkeys from different mountains to serve Rama. Now Sugriva was afraid to meet Lakshmana as he had neglected his duty. Vali's wife Tara was sent for by Sugriva to pacify Lakshmana. Tara came to the gate and saluted Lakshmana. She spoke politely to the brother of Rama, saying, "Lakshmana, your devotion to Rama is incomparable. We are monkeys. We commit so many faults all the time. Be compassionate toward us. It is true that Sugriva indulged in pleasures of the world to the total forgetfulness of his promise to Rama. Now he has come to his senses and is ready to serve you and Rama. Please do not be furious and bless us with inspiration to serve Sri Rama."

Words spoken with calm dignity solve many problems that arise through anger.

Led by Tara, Lakshmana came to Sugriva's palace. Sugriva fell at the feet of Lakshmana and craved forgiveness. In the presence of Lakshmana, Sugriva took the pledge again that he will never rest until the search for Sita is over. Then and there he ordered important monkey chieftains to send word to all the monkey troops from different mountains to gather in Kishkinda. Accordingly, the messengers of Sugriva conveyed the message to all the monkeys, and millions of them, being the part manifestations of celestials who had incarnated to serve Rama, came to Kishkinda. Headed by Sugriva and Lakshmana, the *vaanaras* came to Sri Ramachandra chanting, "Sri Rama Jaya Rama Jaya Jaya Rama." Sugriva fell prostrate at the feet of Rama and renewed his friendship with the pledge. He said, "God, my Lord, ignorant monkey as I am, I was led astray by my monkey mind into the morass of creature comforts. Blessed Lord as you are, forgive me and allow me to serve you. Rama, salutations." Sri Rama blessed him and at the advice of Rama and Lakshmana, Sugriva ordered his troop, thus, "Vinata, take a few million monkeys with you and search for Sita in all eastern directions. Sushena, let millions of monkeys under your leadership go in search of Sita in the western directions. Let Shatabali search in northern regions accompanied by millions of monkeys. As we have the clue that Ravana's Lanka is in the southern direction, let Hanuman, Angada, Jambavan, Mainda, and Dvivida, accompanied by millions of monkeys, search for Sita in that direction. We will never know where the ten-headed demon has hidden Sita. Let all monkeys understand this stipulation. Within a month, you have to come back and report about Sita. If you are indolent and neglect your duties and come later than the specified time, you will be mercilessly punished. Beware of this."

Both Sugriva and Sri Rama felt that Hanuman would certainly accomplish the task. Capable of taking any form, intelligent, totally devoted to Sri Rama, strong and courageous, Hanuman is the greatest among all seventy-two million monkey chieftains; therefore, Sri Rama called him near and handed over his ring in his hand, saying, "O beloved son of wind god, your devotion to me and Sita is unfathomable. I feel you will bring good news about Sita. When you meet her, hand over this ring to her. By this, she will know that you are my messenger." Hanuman was very much inspired by the words of his Master. Hanuman became confident that Rama's grace would make him accomplish the task.

Receiving the blessings from Rama and Lakshmana, the powerful monkeys, with devotion to Rama, began their search for Sita. Searching in every nook and corner of the eastern direction and finding no clue of Sita, Vinata returned with his monkey troop. He submitted the report to Sugriva that they had searched for Sita in almost every cave of the mountains and forests. After a while, Sushena, with his troop, returned from the western direction. He reported to Sugriva that their thorough search brought only this result, that Sita was not to be found anywhere in the western regions. After some time, Shatabali returned with his troop and reported all their efforts were futile for they could not find Sita in the northern regions.

Those who had begun their search in the southern region underwent various experiences. Hanuman, Angada, Jambavan, and others explored the great Vindhya mountains. They were very tired, hungry, and thirsty. They could not find water to drink. Finally, they found a few birds flying out of a cave with wet wings. This made them feel that there should be a water place inside the cave. Without any consideration, all those monkeys entered inside the cave. They were wonderstruck to see very beautiful palaces and gardens inside the cave. They quenched their thirst by drinking lots of water and satisfied their hunger by eating lots of fruits. To their wonder, they could not find the way out. They could not find how many days and nights they had spent there. Finally, Hanuman burst into anger and roared, "Whosoever is the head of this place, let that person appear before me, as we need to go for Rama's service. Any impediment to Rama's *seva* will not be tolerated."

Hearing his roar, a shining woman ascetic, wrapped with bark garments, appeared before them. She asked them who they were and why they entered that place. Hanuman said, "We are the servants of Rama. As his wife Sita has been stolen by the ten-headed demon Ravana, we are searching for Sita in every mountain and cave. Exploring the whole Vindhya mountain, all of us became very thirsty and hungry. It was by seeing a few swans and geese flying out from the cave with wet wings, we thought there should be enough fruits and water available for us. We are completely satisfied as we have had enough fruits and water. Our chief, Sugriva, has given us only a month's time. We do not know how much time we spent here. Please tell us who you are and who this beautiful palace belongs to and tell us whether Ravana has hidden Rama's wife here." Hearing the words of Hanuman, the female ascetic said, "O great servant of Rama, my name is Swayamprabha. This place is illumined only by my presence, and not by the sun, moon, or stars. This palace and garden is built by Maya, the demon sculptor, for his pleasure. I assure you, Sita is not here and no one other than the birds can go out of this cave if they once enter. As you are Lord's servants, our magic never works before you, but still I would request all of you to close your eyes, and within a minute you will all be outside the cave." Those millions of monkeys closed their eyes as they were eager to get out of the cave, and to their amazement, within a minute, they were all taken out by the magic of that ascetic. Thanking her, Hanuman and his troop went in search of Sita and to their utter dissatisfaction, they found that only one day of the month's period given to them was left.

Seeing the vast, blue ocean, they were very much digusted as there was no possibility for any one of them to go across the ocean in search of Sita. Angada called all the monkeys near him and said, "O brothers, in only one day's time we have to accomplish our task. This is simply impossible. Cruel Sugriva, unhesitatingly shall punish us by cutting our limbs or torturing us. Instead of dying such a torturous death, why do not we decide to just sit here, meditating on Rama, and put an end to our lives by fasting until death." All the other tired monkeys agreed to Angada's proposal except Hanuman. Hanuman said, "Angada and all brothers, this is a wrong decision. This is unworthy of the servants of the Lord. Do not be disheartened. Nothing is impossible for the Lord's servants. We have to take shelter in Rama's name and he will show us some way to accomplish our task. Therefore, let us sing the *kirtana* of the Lord and let his miracle show us the way to accomplish our task." Saying thus, Hanuman inspired everybody to chant the Holy Name of Sri Rama.

Nearby, on Mahendra mountain, a huge bird named Sampati was sitting, whose wings had been burnt. Seeing the large number of monkeys sitting together, that huge bird wanted to eat all of them. It came walking near them, and at that time it heard the chanting of the Holy Name of Rama. Even though the bird never knew who Rama was, it also participated in chanting the Holy Name. To its astonishment, it saw its burnt wings growing back again–its full grown wings being miraculously restored by chanting the name of Rama. The bird, which had come to eat the devotees of Rama, itself became a devotee. Such is the efficacy of the Holy Name, which heals everybody who chants or meditates on it. Wondering at the miracle, bird Sampati questioned Angada whose name they were chanting, who they were, and on what mission they were there.

"O bird, Sri Rama, the son of Dasharatha, born of Solar race, was exiled to the forest by his stepmother," Angada replied. "While he was living in the forest with his brother Lakshmana and spouse Sita, some demon stole away Sita. Rama destroyed Vali and installed Sugriva on the throne of Kishkinda and Sugriva is our chief. Pledged to serve Sri Rama by searching for the whereabouts of Sita, Sugriva has sent us to explore Vindhya mountain and southern regions. We searched everywhere and now we are here and have decided to die of hunger. On one hand, we feel if we return without good news about Sita then we will be punished by Sugriva, but on the other, Rama is very compassionate, who blessed another great bird like you named Jatayu, who fought with a demon and lost his wings. We were told that the merciful Rama blessed that bird with pure devotion to Him and with His immortal Kingdom of Heaven. So, merciful Rama will not punish us nor allow Sugriva to punish us."

Hearing these words, Sampati was overwhelmed with

grief. He said, "O *vaanaras*, Jatayu was my youngest brother. When both of us were young, we wanted to race one another to find out who could fly higher than the other. My younger brother Jatayu reached near the sun, and out of affection for him, I decided to protect him from the sun's scorching rays, and soaring higher than he, I spread out my wings above his body. At that very moment, both of my wings were reduced to ashes by the rays of the sun and I fell on this Mahendra mountain. From that day onward, I couldn't fly anymore and used to eat whatever came my way. I have never heard, after falling on the mountain, what happened to my brother Jatayu. After so many years, today for the first time, I am hearing about Jatayu. I am happy he sacrificed his life for Rama. I myself have seen the miracle of Rama which has restored my wings; therefore I also would like to serve Rama in a small way.

"O brothers, while I was sitting on this mountain, one day I saw a celestial lady taken away by a demon in his aerial car. As I was very high on the mountain, I could very clearly see her and the ten-headed demon. As I was very hungry, I stretched my beak to devour both of them but the demon implored me to leave him alive. Thank God. Along with the demon I would have eaten Sita, also, as I knew not who she was. Had I known that Jatayu was deceived by the demon, I would have crushed him out of existence by my beak and restored Sita to Sri Rama. Anyway, I am sure that demon was Ravana from Lanka. If anyone among you can go across the ocean of eight hundred miles and reach Lanka, you will be able to search for Sita there. May the blessings of Rama be on all of us and may your mission be successful." Saying thus, Sampati flew to the mountain top with tears of joy.

Jambavan, the eldest among the monkeys, led all of them to the shores of the ocean. He called a few of the most powerful monkeys and asked them how much of the ocean they could cover and which one of them would be able to reach Lanka. One great monkey chieftain called Gaya said that if he tried, he could perhaps jump a hundred miles. Another monkey named Gavaksha said he could take a leap up to two hundred miles. The third one, Sharabha, said three hundred miles. Vrishabha said four hundred miles. Gandhamadana said five hundred miles. Mainda assured Jambavan he could reach up to six hundred miles. Dvivida said he hoped to cover up to seven hundred miles. The strong monkey, Sushena, hoped to fly up to eight hundred miles, but he was not sure of his strength to fly back. Angada said he could only cover four hundred miles. Finally, Jambavan said, "Friends, I was born of Creator Brahma in Krita Yuga, the Golden Age, and now it is Treta Yuga, the Silver Age. You can imagine how old I am. Still, I feel that I can take a leap up to three hundred miles. How I wish I had enough strength to serve Rama. As I cannot see anyone, among millions of monkeys, able to fly across the ocean and accomplish the work of Rama, I can only think of our beloved Hanuman who is sitting away from us, meditating on Rama. I think that devotee of Rama will certainly be able to do everything and return in time. But friends, when Hanuman was a boy, his pranks disturbed the sages so they cursed him, saying that he should not know his own strength. Then the merciful sages, at the request of his father, softened the curse by telling he will realize his strength only when he is reminded of his strength by others; therefore, I deem it fitting that all of us should glorify Hanuman's strength and then he will perform miracles. This is known only to me and fortunately, by the will of Rama, I am here to tell you this secret." Saying thus, Jambavan approached Hanuman with all other monkeys and began glorifying him. "O beloved Hanuman, you are the greatest servant of the Lord. Lord Rama has blessed you with his ring and his grace to return victorious after finding Sita. O foremost among the monkeys, your accomplishments are endless.

You have a diamond body which is indestructible. You are the son of wind god; therefore, you are capable of flying any distance in a very short time. You are very clever and are capable of knowing the minds of others. Therefore, none will be equal to you in knowing the secret of the demons and assuming the form of your choice while you are in the demon's palace. Why are you silent? Just realize your strength. Awake and arise, O scourge of your foes. Let everybody know the story of Hanuman.

"Hanuman's father was a monkey king named Kesari and his mother's name was Anjani. Having no children for a long time, she sought the advice of Sage Matanga. The sage gave her *Vayu-mantra* and sent her to the sacred seven hills where she meditated. As she was very well-known for her beauty and pleased with her prayers, Vayu, the wind god, blessed her with a strong, intelligent boy. He assured her she need not be afraid of being blessed by him with a son, for this son would be an ever-living servant of the Lord who would relieve all fears of humanity. The boy was named Anjaneya, being the son of Anjani. When he was a child, he took a leap to the solar system, mistaking the sun to be a ripe fruit. He plucked the sun and was about to eat it. Seeing this, *devas* were terrified and they complained to Indra. Indra angrily hit Anjaneya by his thunderbolt, which fractured his jaw. Thereafter, he was known as Hanuman, meaning 'one whose jaw is fractured.' His father, the wind god, stopped blowing out of anger at Indra. All the worlds suffocated. Thereupon, Brahma the creator blessed Hanuman to become invincible in war and no weapon other than Brahma's missile could harm him and even the missile of Brahma could bind him only for a moment and then he would be released. Therefore, friends, you should know that our beloved Hanuman is invulnerable."

Turning toward Hanuman, Jambavan said, "Hanuman, this leaping across the ocean is nothing for you. Even as Lord Vishnu, in his fifth incarnation as Vamana, measured the fourteen worlds with two strides, similarly, you will cover the whole ocean within no time. O all-powerful one, if the demons in Lanka try to capture you or kill you, we are sure that they will be destroyed by your powerful fist and we have no doubt that you will search for Sita, convey her the message of Rama, hand over the ring of the Lord, and teach the ten-headed demon an unforgettable lesson. We, your friends, will be praying for you and your success. The time is very short and we have to get back to Sugriva with the message of Sita. Bless you, O foremost among the monkeys, the knower of the *Vedas*, the greatest *dasa* of Rama. Awake! Arise!"

Hearing these words of Jambavan and millions of his friends, Hanuman realized his own strength. Inspired as he was by Jambavan, he began growing to the size of Mahendra mountain. Raising both of his hands, Hanuman, of indomitable energy, roared thus, "Hear, all celestials, *siddhas*, angels, semigods and demigods. Hear, all *yakshas* and *rakshasas*, hear, all *vaanaras*, I am the servant of Lord Rama, Hanuman, of indefatigable energy. Even eagle Garuda, the vehicle of Vishnu, cannot stand in comparison with me in velocity. By the grace of Sri Rama, easily I shall go across the ocean and search for Janaki. I am positive that I shall see Sita, give her the ring of Rama and convey his message, and return with Sita's message. Among all, I am specially blessed by Rama to accomplish this task. Lifting Meru mountain, uprooting the Himalayas, devouring the planets, are all play for me. Let it be known to all the fourteen worlds that while I am engaged in the service of Rama, if anyone disturbs me, I shall crush them out of existence. If the earth comes to rescue Ravana, I shall pull that planet up and toss it into space. If the sun comes to rescue Ravana, I shall finish him. If Shiva or Brahma or any *devata* try to help Ravana, I will drive them away from their abodes, as *dharma* is on my side. I can dry the ocean, pluck the planets, and do anything to serve my Lord Rama. Let it be known, therefore, that I am the servant of the Lord, and will accomplish the mission for which I was sent.

"O brothers, in a little time you may see me floating in the sky and disappearing from your sight within a twinkling of an eye. Wait until I return. Pray and meditate. May the blessings of Rama be on all of us." Saying thus, Hanuman took a leap over Mahendra mountain and stood like another mountain, kissing the skies. Pledged to the vow of celibacy, that immortal servant of Rama illumined the whole world with his brilliance. His uplifted tail created a halo of "Om" around his head and his crest jewel eclipsed hundreds of suns. Holding the mace in his hand, that immortal Maruti, the son of wind god, stood there to show the universe there is nothing impossible to a servant of the Lord.

Whosoever reads or listens to this episode is rid of all sins and attains transcendental peace. Here ends the fourth book, entitled *Kishkinda Kanda*.

BOOK V

SUNDARA KANDA

Hanuman, the son of wind god, with joined palms, prayed to Sri Ramachandra, Sita, and Lakshmana and offered his prayers to his father, Vayu, and Brahma, Vishnu, and Shiva. He saluted all the guardian deities and as a preparation to fly across the ocean, he pressed both of his palms to Mahendra mountain. Swinging his body to and fro, he made the whole earth rock like a cradle. With a roar that cracked the very shell of the cosmic egg, the mighty servant of Rama leapt across the ocean with outstretched arms. As Hanuman was floating above the clouds, he looked like a flying mountain. Chanting the Holy Name of Rama, that all-powerful son of wind traveled without effort.

As he was flying with great velocity, he saw a mountain coming up from the ocean as if to stop him. Hanuman struck the mountain with his powerful fist, whereupon the mountain god cried, saying, "O Hanuman, please understand that I am a great friend of your father. My name is Mainaka mountain. Listen with patience. In previous times, all mountains had wings. It was Indra who began cutting the wings of the mountains with his thunderbolt. When Indra was chasing me to destroy me, it was your father, Vayu, who hurriedly brought me to the ocean king and protected me from the thunderbolt of

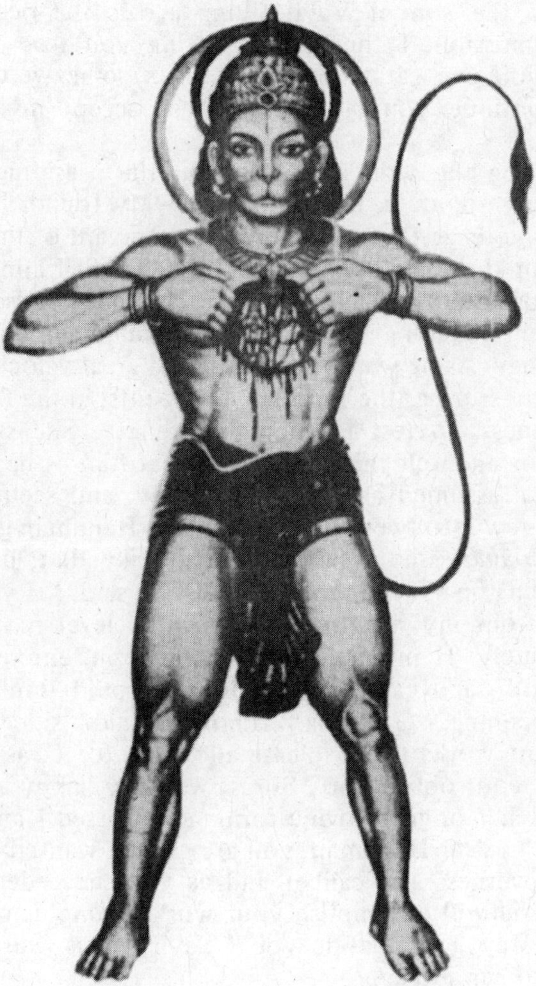

Lord Hanuman

Indra. From that day onward, I was waiting for an opportunity to serve your father through some way. As you are the son of Vayu flying across the ocean on Rama's mission, I thought of letting you rest on me, where you can eat some fruits, drink some water, and then continue your journey. Please accept my hospitality."

Hearing the words of Mainaka, the presiding deity over that mountain, Hanuman said, "My friend, I thank you for your gesture. But how can a servant of the Lord rest until the Lord's work is finished? Still I appreciate your hospitality." Saying thus, Hanuman blessed the mountain, touching it by his hand, and then continued his journey. As he was proceeding with great velocity, the *devas* sent Surasa, the mother of serpents, in the form of a demoness, to test Hanuman's strength. She stopped Hanuman and told him she would eat him as her food. Hanuman assumed a ten *yojanas* body, and seeing this, Surasa grew into twenty *yojanas*. When Hanuman grew to thirty *yojanas*, she grew into forty. Like that, both of them went on growing until finally she said, "If you can escape from my mouth, I call you a clever monkey." Immediately, Hanuman took a teeny form, entered into her mouth, and came out before she could think what was happening. "O Surasa," Hanuman said, "since I have important works to do, please allow me to go, as I have fulfilled your obligation." Surasa was very happy and she assumed her original divine form. She blessed Hanuman, saying, "O dear Hanuman, you are great. I wanted to test your cleverness and caliber and as you succeeded, that means you will accomplish your work among demons in Lanka. May good betide you." Saying thus, Surasa returned to her abode.

Surmounting all difficulties, blessed Hanuman, with all seriousness, made his way toward Lanka. As he was proceeding at a very great height, all of a sudden, he felt suffocated and could not move further, however he tried.

Carefully, he looked in all directions, but he could not find anyone. He remembered the words of Sugriva who had told him about a terrible demoness named Simhika, who catches people by their shadow. So Hanuman carefully looked below and saw that demoness floating on the waters of the ocean, swallowing his shadow. Her body was spread over forty miles by its length, and by its width nearly thirty miles. Hanuman challenged her with his strength and she widened her jaws to swallow him. Instantaneously, Hanuman assumed a teeny form, entered into her stomach, and tearing her bosom, he killed her. *Devas* showered flowers on Hanuman and wished him all success in his endeavor.

Thereafter, that immortal devotee of Sri Ramachandra took a long leap to reach Lanka. But later he found himself in an unknown place and to find out where he was, he approached the hermitage nearby where a great sage named Trinabindu was meditating. Assuming the form of a small monkey, Hanuman saluted his feet and asked him, "O divine master, please tell me how far is Lanka from here and where is that ten-headed demon Ravana dwelling? I have very important work there with that wretched demon and if you show the way, it will really bring you great merit."

Hearing these words of Hanuman, that *yogi* slowly opened his eyes and said, "O small monkey, why are you disturbing my meditation? Even as a blind man requesting a mirror to see his face, and a deaf man desiring to hear divine music, and a lame man expecting to walk in pilgrimage centers; similarly, you, a silly monkey, are desirous of going to Lanka. Ravana is an all-powerful demon, having his golden Lanka over the mountains named Trikuta. There are seven forts encircling the main palace of that demon and in all the forts there are *rakshasas*, evil spirits, ghosts, and different types of demons. Day and night they keep a watch over those forts so that not even a mosquito is allowed to enter into

Lanka. Futile is your effort, O monkey, to reach Ravana's palace. Why don't you be happy just eating fruits and jumping from tree to tree?" Hanuman smiled and said, "O sage, I have come for the work of my Master. It is said in the scriptures that if a man dies for the sake of his teacher and his cause, he automatically reaches the higher heavens; therefore, all that I expect from you is to show me the way to the city of Lanka." Then the old sage said, "O monkey, even though I want to show you the way toward Lanka, don't you see that I cannot even get up from meditation? I have been sitting here since many decades in this lotus posture and my nails have taken their roots into the soil, as have my matted locks. It is possible for me to show you the way, provided you have enough strength to lift me." Now Hanuman thought of showing his strength to the *yogi* and within a twinkling of an eye, assuming a huge form, he plucked the sage from the earth, even as one plucks a fruit from a tree, and held him on his palm to the sky. Realizing the strength of Hanuman, the frightened *yogi* immediately showed the way to the city of Lanka. Seeing this divine form of Hanuman, Brahma, Rudra, and all the celestials were amazed. Leaving the sage in his *ashram*, that sagacious monkey took a leap to the tower of the city of Lanka. It was exactly midnight.

The moon was bright and according to Tulasidas' Ramayana, it was the eleventh day of the bright fortnight known as Ekadashi. The golden Lanka was shining in that moonlight and Hanuman was very happy that he at last reached the place where Sita could be found. He found out that what the sage said was true. There were so many goblins, fiends, and evil spirits, trying to stop him, but Hanuman, by the power of chanting Ramanama, drove them all away.

As he was about to enter the main gate of the city of Lanka, after having crossed the seven forts, he saw a huge demoness standing at the gate, guarding it. Hanuman, assuming a teeny monkey form, wanted to jump across her shoulders to enter into the palace. She roared and held him by the hand and when Hanuman bit her hand, she flung him onto the earth, saying, "Hey *vaanara*, when the entire city is sleeping and all are taking rest, who are you, an insignificant monkey, jumping about here?" Jokingly, Hanuman said, "O terrible demoness, when all are sleeping, why are you standing like a wall near this gate instead of taking rest? What is your job here in this city?" Angrily, the demoness said, "O monkey, if you were clever enough, you would have definitely known who I am. The very fact of my standing near the main gate shows that I am here being the spirit of Lanka, standing to guard this city. Therefore, I am honored and well-known as Lankini. You, O thief, you wanted to escape from me. I am going to crush you between the teeth and make a meal of you." Hanuman burst into laughter and said, "O wretched demoness, I am not a thief. I am the chief among the devotees of Rama and I am the life breath of the whole universe. I am the son of wind god. They call me Hanuman. I am deathless. How can you, mortal fiend, destroy me?"

Hearing these insulting words, the ogress became wild and said, "O silly ape, what does it matter to me if you are Hanuman? Do you have three eyes like Shiva? I am so hungry to eat you and to drink your blood to my heart's content." Saying thus, the demoness tried to catch Hanuman. Escaping her grip, the diamond-bodied one showed his fist and said, "O demoness Lankini, the abode of death is waiting to welcome you and I am going to send you there immediately. If you want to hold your neck on your trunk, without a whisper get out of my way." Lankini could no more bear these insulting words. She discharged severe blows on the body of Hanuman. The diamond-bodied one, to cut her story short, finished her with just one blow over her head. With a cry that shook the whole Lanka City, demoness Lankini fell like a mountain. From her body, there emerged a celestial lady who saluted Hanuman and said, "O immortal devotee of Sri Rama, you have resurrected me. I am the spirit of wealth, who fell as a gatekeeper of Ravana's Lanka due to a curse uttered by Brahma. He also rescinded the curse by saying when you come into contact with Hanuman, he will end your curse of remaining in this demoness body and you will return to your abode. I am grateful to you, O son of wind god, for your mercy of releasing me from this terrible body." Saying thus, that spirit of wealth returned to her abode.

While entering the palace, Hanuman was very careful to place his left leg first because he knew that according to the scripture, in an enemy's camp or palace, it is the left leg which is to be kept first and in a friend's home, the right, Hence, all military armies use, in their marching, "Left, right!"

Hanuman entered into the palaces of many demons such as Mahodara, Mahaparshva, Narantaka, Vajradamstra, Akampana, etc., and was frustrated by not finding Mother Sita in any of those abodes. He saw hundreds and thousands of demons and demonesses, some dreaming, some screaming, some drinking, some wallowing in the pastures of sense pleasures, and some sleeping soundly. By the light of the ring of Rama, Hanuman entered into the inner apartments of demons, even in the midst of darkness, and being a *brahmachari*, with the strict vow of continence, and by the grace of Rama, despite all the young women whom he saw, his mind was not even slightly disturbed. Then he saw a huge hall from where a tumultuous noise was coming. Doubting that Sita might be there, Hanuman, with his teeny monkey form, entered into that hall and suddenly found himself in the nostril of a terrible demon and after a while, when the demon exhaled, he was thrown miles and miles away. Again, while he was inhaling, Hanuman entered into the nostril of the demon, only to come out while he exhaled. Other various huge animals were also suffering in the same way. These annoying nasal trips disgusted Hanuman, who thought of a device of escape for this terrible *karma*. As he went inside the nostril with his teeny form, he grew into a huge size. When he came out, by the force of exhalation, Hanuman's body was dashed to a diamond pillar in that hall; but being himself a diamond-bodied one, Hanuman remained unhurt. As there was no one with whom he could share his joy, other than those unfortunate animals who were caught in the nasal trips, Hanuman burst into laughter, marveling, "Hey Rama, how many kinds of demons are existing in this Lanka? This should be Ravana's brother, Kumbhakarna."

As Hanuman proceeded from that palace to the next palace, he heard a beautiful *harikirtan*. Immediately, Hanuman knew that this should be the abode of Ravana's youngest brother, Vibhishana, the great devotee of Rama. According to Tulasidas' Ramayana, Hanuman assumed the form of a priest and entered into his palace. It is said that even the parrots in Vibhishana's palace were chanting, "Rama, Rama", and Vibhishana welcomed the priest and said, "O great soul, it is so wonderful to have your *darshan* on this most auspicious day of Ekadashi. Never have I come across anyone like you in this city of Lanka. Just by your presence, you have invoked in me great love for the lotus feet of Rama. You should be a great *haridasa*, or who knows, Rama himself might have come in your form to bless me." Thereafter, Hanuman narrated the beautiful story of Rama and revealed that he was Hanuman, and told about his mission in Lanka. Vibhishana, shedding profuse tears of joy, said, "Hey Hanuman, if all the heavenly bliss is placed on one side of a scale, and the bliss of *satsang* on the other, it cannot stand in comparison. Tonight, after many years, I realized how much Lord Rama loves me, for unless the grace of Rama is there, one will never meet his servants." Saying thus, Vibhishana saluted Hanuman.

Searching for Sita in different palaces, finally Hanuman entered Ravana's palace. Beholding the beauty of that palace, Hanuman was wonderstruck. The interior decoration with silver, gold, and diamonds, with rare artwork, was marvelous. The palace was filled with fragrance and music. In the palace of Ravana, Hanuman saw his Pushpaka Vimana, or the aerial chariot. It contained the artwork of birds, serpents, and flowers made of coral, silver, gold, and emerald. Hanuman searched for Sita inside the aerial car.

That aerial car, prepared by the divine sculptor, Vishwa-Karma, was given by Brahma to Kubera. Later, Ravana drove Kubera away by taking Pushpaka Vimana from him. After seeing this wonderful chariot, Hanuman entered into the bed-chamber of Ravana. Hanuman saw the demon sleeping like a huge mountain, his dark body shining due to the rich diadem on his ten heads. There on his left side, Hanuman saw a celestial lady sleeping. For a moment he began beating his forehead, wondering how the chaste wife of Rama could sleep on the bed of the sinful Ravana.

Mistaking that lady for Sita, Hanuman cried bitterly, saying, "Hey Rama, how pure you are! Day and night you remember Sita and you weep for her, but here I see Sita sleeping near Ravana on his bed. Did you send me, Sri Rama, to see this evil sight? How shall I convey to you this bad news? Shall I kill this wretched demon right away, as he has spoiled the mind of Sita and many other women? I have not obtained your permission to do that. I cannot bear this sight." Saying thus, Hanuman cried bitterly. After a while, that sagacious monkey remembered the description of marks over the face and feet of Sita, as explained by Rama. He carefully watched the face and feet of the woman. He found signs of widowhood on her face. But Rama had told him that Sita had the crescent moon mark on her forehead, symbolizing her immortality. Then he observed the feet of that sleeping woman and he could not find the fish mark over the right foot which Sita had. Now he understood that the woman was Mandodari, the wife of Ravana, and not Mother Sita. Hanuman began slapping his own mouth for the wrong words he used about Sita and cried, "O Mother Sita, forgive me for my ignorance, for I am just a monkey. Forgive me."

He couldn't find Sita anywhere. This worried him very much. Now he decided to extend his body and tail, wrap his tail around the Trikuta mountain, pull out the whole mountain, take it to Rama and place it before him to let him search for his beloved Sita himself. Thinking thus, Hanuman wrapped his tail around the Trikuta mountain. Singing the name of Rama, that illustrious monkey began pulling the Trikuta mountain, over which the city of Lanka was built. The entire Lanka began trembling and the wind-god thought of giving proper advice to his son Hanuman. He said, "Hanuman, you have not searched for Sita in the Pushpaka grove. Search there and you will find her. Give up this futile attempt."

Hearing the words of his father, Hanuman assumed a small form and jumping from tree to tree, he reached the Ashoka grove. He saw Sita sitting under the foot of Shimshupa tree. He sat above the tree and began observing what was happening. From the tree he saw Sita surrounded by many demonesses. Some had one eye, some had four eyes, some had three arms, some had four legs, some had three ears and two noses and tusks. Among these terrible looking female titans, Sita was shining like a cow among tigers, parrot among crows, rose among thorns, moon among clouds. He saw them harassing Sita by constantly demanding for her to consent to the wishes of Ravana. Sita was silently shedding profuse tears of grief and was not sipping even a drop of water. When Hanuman saw that Mother of the Universe, embodiment of chastity, personification of purity, he was beside himself with joy because he had the *darshan* of the spouse of

Rama. He sat as a small monkey on the top-most branch of the tree, hiding among the leaves, silently observing.

Stormed and agitated by lust, the ten-headed demon, washing and decorating himself with rare jewels and surrounded by many demons and demonesses who were holding burning torches in their hands, approached Sita. At that hour of the night, sitting on a comfortable seat in the garden, that mountainous-bodied demon sent Vibhishana's wife Sarama and his daughter Trijata to find out if Sita had changed her mind to accept the will of Ravana.

After a while, Sarama and Trijata returned from Sita with this message. They said to Ravana, "O king, Sita has no thought other than Rama. Night and day she meditates on Rama. Rama is her everything. Lotuses may blossom out of rock, jasmine flower may give up its fragrance, but Sita will never swerve her mind from Rama. Flies may swallow a mountain, ants may drink an ocean, but it is not possible for Sita to swerve her mind from Rama. Cats may grow horns, sugar may give up its sweetness, but Sita can never swerve her mind from Rama. Sun and moon may change their directions of rising and setting, earth may revolve in the opposite position, but Sita can never swerve her mind from Rama."

Hearing this message Ravana flew into a rage. Now he himself approached Sita. He placed a box of ornaments before her and spoke thus, "O beautiful Sita, your moon-like face is eclipsed by your worries and anxieties. When you are the queen of Lanka, why should you worry? All my other queens will be your maidservants. I myself am your servant. These ten heads, which have never bent before anyone, I bend at your feet and pray, O benevolent lady, kindly shower your grace on me and become my queen. I am scorched by the sharp arrows of cupid. I am peaceless and unhappy without you. Sita, use your intelligence; Rama can never come to Lanka. In this life you can never see him again. By this time Rama might have already died. He is a beggar. He has no kingdom, palaces, or riches. Loving him, what will you get? Here you can enjoy the whole palace, whatever you desire is instantaneously brought to you. Give up this thought of Rama. Wash your face, fix your hair, deck your neck with ornaments of your choice. This garden is built to remove all sorrows of people who are scorched by grief. Therefore, it is named as Ashoka grove which means the grove that relieves one from all sorrows. Even though you sit here in this beautiful garden, still you are always filled with grief. Enjoy the beauty of this garden, forget Rama and Lakshmana, marry me, and become the queen of Lanka."

Hearing these lustful words of the arrogant demon, Sita's face and eyes turned red out of anger and she plucked a blade of grass which she kept in front of her to divide her from the demon. Without looking at the demon, she addressed him through the blade of grass. There are various symbolic meanings for her placing the grass before the demon:

1. The grass separates the vibration of Ravana which cannot overpower Sita.
2. Sita considered Ravana as a blade of grass before Rama.
3. Sita considered all the wealth of Ravana as a blade of grass before the wealth of true love for Rama.
4. Sita wanted the demon to know that even as the fire reduces the grass into ashes by its touch, similarly, the fire of her austerity would burn Ravana if he tried to touch her.
5. Ravana, along with all the demons, is like a blade of grass, and will be destroyed by Rama, who is like a fire.
6. As Ravana had come at that late hour of night with an animal instinct, Sita kept the grass, treating

Ravana as an animal, for him to eat the grass and go away.

She addressed Ravana through the blade of grass, thus, "O wretched Ravana, because you came disguising yourself as a monk, I honored you at the hermitage of Rama. Now through your meanness you are treated like a blade of grass. Where is Rama and where are you? How could there be any comparison between you and he? He is God. You are a demon. He is pure, you are impure. He is like the day and you are like the night. He is like a lion and you are like a goat. He is like a tiger, you are like a fox. You stole me away from Rama. If you were really powerful, why didn't you fight with Rama and vanquish him before you brought me here? How could unrighteousness thrive for a long time? You will definitely meet death by the sharp arrow of Rama. If you want to keep your heads on your trunk, you had better restore me to Sri Rama. Lakshmana's arrows shall destroy the entire Lanka. Do not treat Rama and Lakshmana as ordinary human beings. Give up this folly. Surrender to Rama by taking me back to him. He is the ocean of mercy. He will forgive you. Go away from my presence. Do not stand here anymore, O ten-headed worm."

Hearing these words of Sita, Ravana was very angry. He drew his sword and rushed toward Sita with an intention of killing her. His wife Mandodari stopped him from doing that heinous crime. Ravana returned to his palace, saying, "O Sita, better you behave. Within a month you must marry me; otherwise, I will kill you and satisfy myself by drinking your blood." Saying thus, Ravana returned to his abode.

Sita cried bitterly with great agony. She sobbed saying, "Sri Rama, how can I bear these insults? How long should I suffer like this? When will you come to relieve me from this agony? I can wait no more. Better for me to die rather than live such a painful life of separation from you." As Sita was worrying thus,

Vibhishana's daughter Trijata approached her and consoled her with these words: "Mother Sita, a few minutes ago I had a dream. In this dream I saw Rama and Lakshmana with their monkey chieftains invade Lanka, destroy the demons, and finally, I saw Ravana being destroyed by Rama. With great glory my father Vibhishana offered you back to Rama. Both of you felt great happiness and peace. Sita, this is a true dream. I definitely feel your days of suffering are coming to an end very soon and you will be back with your husband. Please don't worry. Take some rest." Saying thus Trijata returned to her abode.

During the early hours of the morning, seeing all the demonesses at rest, Sita, pained with the pangs of separation, cried very much, "Hey Raghurama," she sobbed, "when will your grace be showered upon me? When will this dark night of my lifetime come to an end? When will this world be free from demons and *dharma* restored? I have no strength anymore to live without you in this kingdom of demons. Once the morning sun rises, then there will again be the harrassment from the demonesses. Rama, let me reach your feet today by killing myself. I have no other way." Saying thus, that immortal daughter of Janaka wrapped her *sari* around her neck and began tightening it.

Hanuman, who was watching from the tree, was perplexed without knowing what to do. If he jumped from the tree, thinking that to be the magic of the demons, Sita would kill herself by tightening the knot around her neck. Should he sit quietly, then also she was going to kill herself. There was no time even to think. All that Hanuman could do at that hour was to sing, "Rama, Rama." Suddenly, Sita looked up to see from where Ramanama was coming. This gave breathing time to Hanuman, and immediately, he began narrating Ramayana to Sita with one breath. "Dasharatha, the king of Ayodhya, who had four children by three queens, out of which Rama and Lakshmana, going with Vishwamitra, killing Tataka, destroying Subahu, tossing Mareecha to Lanka, resurrecting Ahalya, snapping Shiva's bow, marrying Sita, vanquishing Parashurama, exiling themselves to the forest for the fulfillment of the word of promise of their father, blessing Bharata with his sandals, moving to Panchavati, maiming Shoorpanakha, killing fourteen thousand demons along with Khara and Dushana, searching for Sita who was abducted by the demon Ravana, killing Viradha, blessing Jatayu, destroying Kabandha, blessing Shabari, meeting me, Hanuman, destroying Vali, installing Sugriva, sending the *vaanaras* in all four directions, in search of Sita, blessing me with his ring, giving me enough strength to fly across the ocean, that blessed Lord, Sri Ramachandra, showering his grace upon me to come to Lanka, vanquishing Surasa, killing Simhika, destroying Lankini, entering into the nostril of Kumbhakarna, coming out successfully, meeting Vibhishana, entering into the palace of Ravana, seeing the aerial car, coming to the Ashoka grove, sitting on the branch of this Shimshupa tree, one who was watching all that which was happening is the servant of Rama, servant of Sita, Hanuman, Ram, Ram, Ram, Ram!"

Thus, narrating all that had happened with one breath, Hanuman jumped down from the tree assuming a small form and rolled at the dust of the feet of Sita, saying, "O Universal Mother, salutations. O Divine Mother, adorations. O daughter of Janaka, spouse of Rama, *avatar* of Lakshmi, *shakti* of *Treta Yuga*, one who has incarnated to show ideal womanhood and to destroy the demons, through your instrumentality, salutations, salutations. I am Hanuman, son of wind god, servant of Rama, minister of Sugriva. O Mother, after your abduction by Ravana, Rama and Lakshmana met one another, searched for you in the hermitage and throughout the forest, until finally they reached Jatayu. Hearing information of you from him, they proceeded to the *ashram* of Shabari. On the way, Kabandha gave them some information and Shabari told them about Sugriva and monkeys. Rama came to the bank of Pampa, and there he accepted me as his *dasa*. Today, by his grace, I am here, O Mother.

"Hey Janaki, with my own eyes I have seen and heard the chastisement and abusive epithets of the ten-headed demon. The most difficult period of your life has come to an end. Worry no more."

Hearing the words of Hanuman, Sita felt a great joy and peace for the first time since her abduction. She told Hanuman, "Hanuman, your words are very soothing. Due to living in a demon's kingdom, my mind is filled with doubts and fear. I don't understand how a teeny monkey like you can fly across the ocean and how you can seek me in all palaces and come here alive. Mareecha, through his magic, appeared to me as a golden deer and brought all this calamity. I hope you are not a demon playing the monkey. Forgive me for my fear and give me some clue that you have come from Rama."

Hanuman said, "O Mother Sita, if you want to see my true form with which I flew across the ocean, with your permission I will reveal it." Saying thus, Hanuman covered the whole space with his diamond body. Sita was astonished to see that Meru mountain-like body and closed her eyes with terror, saying, "Hanuman, assume your small form, please," and then and there Hanuman assumed the form of a teeny monkey. "Now mother, the second and the most precious clue that I am the servant of Rama and have been sent by him is this ring. Please accept this ring of your beloved." Saying thus, Hanuman offered the ring in the hands of Sita.

Sita saw Rama in that ring and bathed the ring with her tears, kissed the ring, feeling Rama in it, and entered into higher states of consciousness. Hanuman felt delighted. Sita blessed Hanuman with tears of joy and asked, "Hanuman, how long should I suffer here? When will my Rama take me back with him?" Hanuman said, "Mother, if you wish, this very moment I can carry you over these shoulders and take you to Rama." Sita said, "Hanuman, you are a *brahmachari* and I am *pativrata*, who has taken the vow not to touch any man other than my Lord, Rama; therefore, I will wait until Sri Rama comes and destroys the demon. Would you kindly tell my beloved Lord that I am living only with the hope of seeing him. Will you kindly convey my heart's love that I do not think or dream of any other than Rama." Hanuman said, "I will, Mother, I will, but I need something to carry just as the ring that Rama gave. Would you kindly give something as a token of your love to Rama, which will make Rama and everybody confident that I have seen you and you have sent your love through the token."

Sita immediately took her crest jewel known as Chudamani and handed it over to Hanuman. Hanuman, holding it, sang, "Sitaram, Sitaram," and leapt and jumped and danced to his heart's content. For Sita, it was a sight to see the monkey jumping and singing the Holy Name. Now Hanuman wanted to play some pranks. He never wanted to run away from Lanka without teaching a lesson to the ten-headed demon. He begged Sita to allow him to eat the fruits from the trees of that Ashoka grove. Sita said, "Hanuman, there are many demons here. I am afraid that they may hurt you, my son. Why not eat only the fruits that have fallen on the ground?" Hanuman smiled and said, "All right, Mother. I will make the fruits fall on the ground and then eat." Saying thus, Hanuman began his pranks. He rooted out hundreds of trees and began hurling them over the demons. He drove off thousands of demons, lashing them by his diamond tail. Demons went and complained to Ravana about the arrival of a monkey that had destroyed Ashoka grove, killing the demons. Ravana was very much upset and he sent a great leader named Jambumali, who was the son of his prime minister, Prahasta. Jambumali hurled thousands of arrows and weapons over Hanuman. Hard as the diamond was his body which no arrows or weapon could penetrate. All the weapons and arrows were like the straw that is thrown into a blazing fire. Hanuman easily destroyed Jambumali along with all his troops. This enraged Ravana and he sent all the sons of his ministers who began an oblation to the blazing fire-like Hanuman. Rocks, mountains, trees, mace, and his fist were his weapons with which he destroyed all who attacked him. He converted hundreds of demons by teaching them Ramanama. Just out of the fear of his tail, the demons began chanting. Otherwise, he would send them to the abode of death. This disgusting news made Ravana become furious and he sent his greatest son, Indrajit, to bring the monkey to the court by chaining him.

Accordingly, Indrajit came with all his chant arrows and began hurling them at the monkey. There is no weapon on earth or heaven which can kill, bind, or hurt Hanuman other than Brahma-astra or the missile of Brahma. Even that can bind him only for a moment and then he is released. Such was the boon of Brahma to Hanuman. Indrajit finally discharged his missile of Brahma. Hanuman also wanted to face Ravana and to admonish him with the words of wisdom; therefore, he made himself captive by Brahma's missile, and Indrajit took it to be a victory and chained Hanuman. He sent ten thousand demons to pull Hanuman, and all those demons could not shake his feet an inch, so they all fell at his feet. Finally, Indrajit sent for thousands of chariots, which Hanuman destroyed by kicking them, until finally, the diamond chariot of Kumbhakarna was brought. He threw himself on the chariot, which millions of demons began pushing and pulling. Thus, it became a grand chariot festival of Hanuman in Lanka. Hanuman was the first ambassador from India to Lanka who spread the word of God in a foreign country thousands of years ago.

Now he came to the court of Ravana. Ravana was sitting on a glorious throne, embellished with gold, rubies, and emeralds. His ten heads were like the ten peaks of the Himalayas. His body was dark as a cloud, over which his ornaments were like lightning. Holding a sword and many celestial weapons in his twenty arms, the king of the titans, seeing monkey Hanuman, burst into laughter. "O silly monkey, how dare you enter into Lanka and destroy Ashoka grove. Who are you? Who sent you? Why have you come? When did you come? Why did you destroy the Ashoka grove and all our troop? Tell everything without any delay." With the coils of his extended tail, Hanuman formed a throne over which he sat, and Hanuman's throne was higher than the throne of Ravana. Now Hanuman spoke. "O Ravana, are you the same one who, disguising himself as a monk, has stolen Sita, the beloved wife of Rama? Shame on you. How many millions of women have you stolen from different *lokas* and made them slaves of your palace? You are a slave to your own desire and had no audacity to face Rama and fight with him and then take Sita with you. O king of titans, I am Hanuman, son of wind god, minister of Sugriva, but more than anything I am the least servant among millions of servants of Rama. I was sent by Rama and Sugriva to search for Sita and I am successful in my mission. I have killed the demons for self-defense. I have destroyed the Ashoka grove where my mother, Sita, is chastised by you. You have read the *Vedas* and you meditate every day. Despite that, you have never realized Rama as Vishnu. It is not too late even now. You can surrender Sita to Rama. To keep Sita here is like keeping burning embers on one's own head. To keep her here is like trying to scratch one's cheeks with a seven-hooded cobra. Ravana, she is your death. She is Maha Lakshmi. If you want to save your heads and the heads of all the demons, come with me, along with Sita, and offer Sita back to Rama. Merciful Rama will certainly bless you and forgive all the wrongs that you have done to Sita. Your unrighteousness will kill you. Protect *dharma* and *dharma* will protect you."

"Strike, strike, strike on his face," cried Ravana. "How dare he teach wisdom to me! Should a serpent teach wisdom to the eagle, and an ignorant man to a man of wisdom, should a monkey teach wisdom to me? O, thousands of my brothers, where have you kept your weapons, as if this was a grand speech. You are all hearing with your ears and eyes wide open, instead of torturing that monkey with the pain of death. Hurry, delay no more. Strike and kill him!" Hearing the words of Ravana, the demons stood up with their swords in their hands, but no one dared approach Hanuman, for they had heard of the prowess of the diamond-bodied monkey.

The sagely Vibhishana intervened at this moment and said to his elder brother Ravana: "O my dear brother, you know the *Vedas* and the scriptures. Even according to political rules of conduct it is not right to kill an ambassador. He is the ambassador of Rama. He has pleaded his case. To accept it or reject it is left to you. For me, what he said seems to be *dharma*. To abduct another's woman is unrighteous. The only way to correct ourselves is to return her to her husband. In any case, Hanuman should not be killed." Immediately, Ravana thought of mutilating his limbs and finally he ordered his people to soak the tail of Hanuman in oil, burn it, and take him in procession with his tail in flames throughout the city of Lanka. This became a big joke to the demons. They brought tons and tons of oil to soak that huge tail, which Hanuman grew longer and longer. There was an oil scarcity in Lanka. Then they began wrapping the cloths. The more it was wrapped, the more Hanuman's tail grew and there was rationing of cloths in Lanka, until finally, they set fire to the end of his tail. The compassionate Mother Sita blessed him from her Ashoka grove. "Let fire be cool to Hanuman," she prayed. So the fire never hurt him. Holding the flaming tail, Hanuman began burning the entire city of Lanka. "Here comes he." Saying thus, thousands of demons and demonesses ran out of their homes and within a few minutes, the entire city of Lanka was in flames. Ravana learned his lesson when the ends of his moustache were burnt by Hanuman's tail. If one monkey servant of Rama could do so much in a short time, what would happen to Lanka and the demons if Rama and Lakshmana came with seventy-two million? Unfortunately, the demon never thought about it.

After burning Lanka, Hanuman felt very sorry. "Oh, monkey I am. For I do not know what happened to Mother Sita due to the entire Lanka burning." Thinking thus, Hanuman jumped into the ocean, put out the fire of his tail and came to see Mother Sita. "Forgive me, O Divine Mother, for my monkey pranks. Bless me. I am going back to Rama." Sita was in tears at parting with such a beautiful *haridasa* who had brought the message of Rama and his ring to her. "Hanuman," she said, "you brought strength and joy to me. You gave me some hope to live in this world. Please tell Rama my love and Lakshmana my blessings. Tell all your friends my blessings. Bring my Lord as soon as possible and relieve me from this pain." Hanuman promised Sita, saying "Devi, your message I shall convey along with your crest jewel. I shall see that Rama, with all of us, will be here very soon to destroy the demons and to relieve you from the clutches of Ravana. Your purity, your blessings, have the power to restore *dharma*. Salutations, embodiment of chastity. Salutations." Saying thus, that illustrious son of wind took a leap across the ocean, with a triumphant victory over the demons, and returned to his friends, who werewaiting miserably on the other side of the ocean. All of them, along with Jambhavan, gave a warm welcome to Hanuman and requested him to recount his doing in Lanka.

Hanuman explained everything in a nutshell and all of

them entered a great garden called Madhuvana and ate a lot of fruits, drank water, and returned to Rama. Hanuman kept within the time duration by bringing the message of Sita within a month. He narrated picturesquely all that happened on his way to Lanka, the trials and tribulations which he faced in Lanka, and his meeting with Sita. Finally, he handed over Chudamani, the crest jewel of Sita to Rama. Rama felt a great peace as if his beloved had returned to him with that token of love. Out of great affection for Hanuman, who brought the two hearts together, Rama embraced him warmly and blessed him thus.

"Hanuman, I am very much indebted to you. Tell me, what boon shall I confer on you?" With joined palms and his eyes bedimmed with tears of joy, Hanuman said, "Prabho, let me have the privilege to serve you and to be at your feet always. Other than this, I care for nothing. Your true love is everything." Sri Rama said, "Hanuman, my love is always with you and you will be at my feet throughout eternity. I want to bless you as the greatest of the *haridasas*. None will come to me but through you. Your heart is my heart and mine yours. You will be the ever-living servant of mine. When the present Brahma completes his cycle and enters into me, I appoint you as the creator for the coming creation. Whosoever reads, recites, sings, and listens to this *Sundara Kanda*, flooded with the divine pastimes of yours, will attain health, wealth, longevity, progeny, and finally my transcendental abode. You will be worshipped by human beings, denizens of heaven, angels, and everybody. You will be the ideal for those who practice devotion, self-surrender, and selfless service. You are most dear to me, O son of wind." Saying thus, Sri Rama blessed him again and again. Celestials showered flowers on Hanuman and Rama.

BOOK VI

YUDDHA KANDA

Sugriva and Hanuman assured Rama and Lakshmana that the *vaanaras* were capable of building the bridge over the ocean and destroying Lanka and the demons. They made all the arrangements for the *vaanaras* to march toward the ocean. At the order of Sugriva, the most powerful monkeys went in different directions to bring mountains, rocks, etc., to help bridge the ocean. Nala, who was an adept engineer, began building the bridge, but unfortunately the ocean began swallowing all the mountains and rocks. Seeing this, Hanuman began writing "Sri Rama Jaya Rama Jaya Jaya Rama" *mantra* over the rocks and mountains and those rocks and mountains, by the power of the Holy Name, never sank, but began to float.

Sri Rama thought of testing his own strength, as his name made the mountains and rocks float. He picked up a small stone and hurled it into the ocean. Instead of floating, it sank. Hanuman saw this and called all the *vaanaras* and began telling them Rama's name is greater than Rama himself. Rama asked Hanuman the reason why the stone which he threw sank while the ones that Hanuman threw were floating. Hanuman replied, "My Lord, the rocks and the mountains that I threw were floating because of the power of your Holy Name, whereas the stone which you threw had nothing to hold it as it was thrown by God. If God throws, there is no one to hold. If God holds, no one can throw." Rama smiled and blessed Hanuman. Thus the efficacy of the Holy Name of God is proved to all men.

Sri Rama appealed to the ocean king, Varuna, to assist the monkeys in building the bridge instead of bringing impediments, but Varuna was stubborn. Fasting, Rama slept on the shores of the ocean so that Varuna would behave, but still he was adamant. "Butter will only melt by the touch of the heat. The ocean king will not melt until I punish him," thought Rama, and discharged a powerful arrow at Varuna. The water of the ocean began boiling and Varuna, with his queens, prayed Rama for forgiveness and to save their lives. Now Varuna realized the greatness of Rama and promised to cooperate with the *vaanaras*.

With great enthusiasm, Nala built the bridge with the help of the *vaanaras*. This news threatened the peace of Lanka. Ravana called a council immediately. He asked the opinion of the *rakshasas* about the course of action to be taken. One after another, all those demons told Ravana not to surrender Sita as they were capable of destroying Rama and *vaanaras*. They said, "Ravana, you are the ruler of the three worlds. Nothing is impossible for you. You have conquered all the celestials. You have lifted Kailasa mountain. You have conquered Kubera and have confiscated this golden city of Lanka and the Pushpaka Vimana from him. All the *devas* are afraid of you. What can this poor man Rama and those monkeys do? Your son, Indrajit, is invincible in the battle and your brother, Kumbhakarna, is invulnerable. Our military is well-trained and well-equipped so there is no cause for anxiety."

Thus, Prahasta, the commander-in-chief, and other *rakshasas* encouraged Ravana to fight the battle with Rama. It was only Vibhishana among the gathered assembly that spoke the truth saying, "O my dear brother, you know what is *dharma* and what is *adharma*. Nobody need teach you. The greatest sin is the abduction of Sita. However powerful we might be, this one sin can destroy our whole race; therefore, I don't think we should fight the battle with Rama. To surrender Sita to Rama is the best course to follow." Ravana was angry and he adjourned the meeting.

The next day, Kumbhakarna was invited by Ravana for his advice. Kumbhakarna was a very fierce demon. No sooner he was born than he began growing in great dimensions and wanted to swallow the whole world. When, by his austerity, he pleased the creator Brahma, he wanted to ask boons to be invincible in battle. At the request of celestials, goddess Saraswati entered into his mind and made him pray for a boon, asking the creator to bless him with six months' sleep and six months' eating. Brahma blessed him with that boon, saying that if you are awakened before the completion of your six months' sleep you will die in a battle. This is the background of Kumbhakarna. He advised his brother with these words, "Ravana, I feel you have done something wrong. If you brought Sita after slaying Rama, that would have been right. Instead, you stole her away and now you want to fight Rama and the *vaanaras*. I don't see any *dharma* in it. Whatever it is, if you insist, even though it means destruction of all the demons, I will certainly be prepared to die for you. Do as you wish."

Vibhishana, the youngest brother of Ravana, spoke frankly once again, "Ravana, the destruction of the race is definite unless you surrender Sita to Rama. Our position is weakened by your unrighteousness. You yourself have seen how one monkey from Rama's army could burn the entire Lanka. In my opinion Rama is God; Sita is Goddess; monkeys are celestials. This is a hidden drama of God for the destruction of the evildoers. Whatever it is, if you offer Rama's wife back to him, this problem is solved. If you hesitate to do this, I can do it for you. With your permission, I can take Sita back to Rama and pray for his forgiveness. I am sure he will forgive us. Please allow me to do that." Hearing these words of Vibhishana, Ravana began burning with anger. "O wretch," he said, "how dare you glorify my enemy in my presence. Don't you know how powerful I am? You have insulted me by praising my enemy. Get out of my sight. If Rama is your God, you have no place in Lanka. Better you go and take refuge in him." Vibhishana said, "Well, if that is your wish, I shall go. None can avert the inevitable. When all the demons are destroyed and your ten heads fall off, then at least you will remember my words that you should have surrendered Sita to Rama. I am going." Saying thus, that immortal devotee of Rama, followed by four of his noble friends, flew in the air to join Rama on the other side of the sea.

Sugriva, Angada, and other monkey chieftains, saw four demons descending to their camp from the sky. A great discussion took place among the monkeys about how to handle the situation. Vibhishana spoke the truth, "O *vaanaras*, I am Vibhishana, the devotee of Rama. I am, of course, the youngest brother of Ravana, but I have renounced Lanka and my brother, and I have come with total surrender to Sri Rama. Please allow me to speak my heart to Rama."

Leaving Vibhishana and his four friends there under heavy guard of *vaanaras*, Jambavan, Sugriva, and others approached Sri Rama and said, "Rama, Vibhishana, the youngest brother of Ravana, has come with four friends to take refuge in you. We doubt in his surrender. We think he has come with wrong intentions of seeing our army and knowing its secrets. We think his four friends to be spies who have come to find out the secret operation of our military and reveal it to Ravana. We have to punish these five people for their intrusion."

Now Rama turned to Hanuman and asked for his opinion. Hanuman said, "My Lord Rama, you know everything. No one need teach you anything, but still you want to ask us so that *dharma* could be reestablished. I have met Vibhishana in Lanka. In my opinion, he is your true devotee. He has come here, breaking his connection with his elder brother Ravana. He has come here as your devotee and friend. In my opinion, he is sincere. But do as you wish, my Lord." Hanuman's speech gave a great joy to Rama. He said to all the *vaanaras*, "O *vaanaras*, even though one is my enemy, if he comes to me and says, 'I have surrendered to you,' then I shall protect him from all danger. Those who surrender to me, I make them fearless. This is my vow.

"Vibhishana has come here with his friends to take refuge in me. I cannot deny such a friend. He has forsaken everything for my sake; therefore, I must receive him in my love. Go and bring him." Sugriva brought Vibhishana and his friends to Sri Rama and Sri Rama received Vibhishana very warmly. Vibhishana glorified Sri Rama, thus, "Rama, O Mahavishnu Avatar, I have surrendered myself to your lotus feet. You are the sole refuge of your votaries. You have come to restore *dharma*. However I try to convince my brother about this truth, he will not listen to me but by your grace, you gave me this true devotion to your lotus feet. I am yours. Accept me and bless me to be your worthy servant."

Pleased with the devotion of Vibhishana, Sri Rama sent Hanuman to bring the holy water from the ocean, and then and there he declared Vibhishana to be the future king of Lanka and sprinkled the holy water over his head. All the *vaanaras* were astonished. They said, "Rama, we have not yet gone across the ocean. Neither have we won the battle with Ravana. How could you declare Vibhishana to be the future king of Lanka? Suppose Ravana, at a future date, comes and surrenders to you like Vibhishana. Then how will you fulfill this promise?" Rama smilingly said, "O *vaanaras*, if Ravana surrenders himself to me, then I shall leave Lanka for him and give my Ayodhya to Vibhishana." *Vaanaras* hailed Rama by telling, "Raghuramachandra Maharaj Ki Jai."

This episode is one of the greatest examples to show the greatness of Rama who accepted the brother of Ravana, the one who had stolen Rama's spouse. This Vibhishana-Sharanagati, or his total surrender to God, is sung by millions of devotees in India every day. Whosoever reads, recites, and listens to this story, realizes the glory of self-surrender and attains peace.

At an auspicious moment, Rama gave his orders to the *vaanaras* to march to Lanka. Hearing about the arrival of Rama's army, Ravana was agitated. He sent two of his messengers named Shuka and Sarana to spy on the monkeys. They were caught by the monkey chieftains and were taken to Rama. When they were about to be punished by the monkeys, the compassionate Rama told the monkeys to forgive them and sent them back to their king, Ravana. Shuka and Sarana came to Ravana and narrated the glory of Rama. They said, "Ravana, even when we were caught by the *vaanaras*, the merciful Rama never allowed them to punish us. We saw innumerable monkey chieftains and the most powerful Lakshmana and Rama. We definitely feel our army will be routed in the battle and the best way to escape from Rama's arrow is to surrender Sita to Rama." Ravana was very angry at them and he returned to his abode.

Out of great desire to attract Sita's mind toward himself, Ravana created an image of Rama, filling life in it with his magical powers. He took the mimicry of Rama to Sita and told her: "O Janaki, at least now you should realize my power. Your husband, who came here to fight, is captured by me, and I have brought him here to sacrifice him as a goat. Tell me now, if you consent to marry me, I will save him; otherwise I am going to kill him." Turning toward that simulated figure of Rama, Ravana insisted, "Come on. Tell her what you want to tell." To her wonder, Sita saw that figure speaking with the voice of Rama, saying, "O Sita, kindly release me from the clutches of Ravana. He is more powerful than I. I give you permission. Please become the queen of Ravana and enjoy the pleasures of Lanka." Sita could not believe such words coming from her Rama. A pure woman as she was, she could not accept what had been said; then, in her presence, Ravana cut off the head of that figure and went away. Sita cried with great agony, holding the head of that figure. In the meantime, Sarama consoled her, saying, "Sita, why have you forgotten the true nature of your Lord and yourself? Don't you know that Rama is God and invincible? There is no cause for despair. I can take you in this airplane and show you your Lord who is very safe." Saying thus, Sarama took Sita in an aerial car and showed her Rama and Lakshmana surrounded by *vaanaras*. Consoling Sita, Sarama returned her to the Ashoka grove.

At the request of Sugriva, Rama climbed Mount Suvela and asked Vibhishana to describe Lanka and Ravana's troops. Vibhishana said, "Rama, the golden Lanka is built on Trikuta mountains by the divine sculptor, Vishwakarma. Ravana usurped the throne of Kubera by driving him away in a fierce battle. Ravana has obtained many boons from Creator Brahma and is invincible in battle. None but you, hey Rama, can conquer him in battle. His brother, Kumbhakarna, also is invulnerable. If he completes his six months' sleep and then stands on the battlefield, he will conquer without any doubt. Ravana's son, Indrajit, has conquered Indra himself and received that boon. He can easily vanquish millions of monkeys unless they are headed by monkey chieftains like Sugriva and Hanuman. Prahasta, the commander-in-chief of the *rakshasa's* army can certainly create a havoc with his arrows. There are many powerful demons like Vajradamstra, Akampana, Mahodara, Atikaya, etc., who have great magical powers, and they can fight in air, water, and earth visibly and invisibly, but

Rama, your one arrow can destroy all these demons and restore *dharma*. Do not worry." As Vibhishana was describing the leaders of Ravana's troop, Sarana began describing to Ravana the leaders of Rama's troop. For this purpose, Ravana climbed his terrace and Sarana, from that height, showed him the ocean of monkeys gathered on the seashore of Lanka. "Look there, Ravana," said Sarana, "One who is standing on Mount Suvela, holding his Kodanda bow in his left hand, with an inexhaustible quiver hanging at his back, that is Sri Rama, the God incarnate, powerful person who can reduce our army to ashes by one arrow. One who is standing to his right holding his bow and arrow is his devoted brother, the invincible Lakshmana. If he becomes angry, he can blow up Lanka. To the left side of Rama you will see commander-in-chief of the *vaanaras*. His name is Sugriva. He is the younger brother of Vali, whom you know. One who is at the feet of Rama is the diamond-bodied Hanuman who taught us a great lesson by burning Lanka. He alone can lift the Trikuta mountain and drown the city of Lanka in the ocean. Then there are very powerful and wise monkey chieftains like Angada, Jambavan, Nala, Neela, etc. Ravana, I have no idea how we will be able to destroy Rama's army." As Sarana was describing thus, Ravana, to insult Rama, hit an arrow in the air. Sugriva was angered at this and he suddenly flew to the terrace where Ravana was standing, kicked him on his head, and returned to Rama safely. Rama advised Sugriva not to take such risks. Insulted by Sugriva, Ravana was much agitated and returned to his palace.

Angada Sandhana

Even though all preparations were made for the warfare, still Sri Rama thought of trying to bring a compromise with Ravana that he would give up war if the demon surrendered Sita. Angada, the son of Vali, was selected for this purpose. Sri Rama blessed him, saying, "My dear Angada, you are as powerful as your father, but today you have to use your intelligence and vocabulary for bringing a compromise between Ravana and I. You should not harm anybody but for self-defense. You should try to speak to the demon and his assembly convincingly and with love. See that you convince them that I have come to restore *dharma* and the abduction of Sita is really unrighteous. Tell them that this is a last opportunity for them to come to a settlement whereby offering Sita back to me, all the wrongs they have done will be forgiven."

Receiving the blessings of Sri Rama, Angada started on his mission and came to the city of Lanka. Seeing Angada, people began running in the streets, telling, "Oh, that monkey which burnt Lanka has come back again. This time he may kill all of us." Then Angada consoled them by saying, "Friends, I am not Hanuman, the one who has burnt Lanka. I am Angada, who has come to convey the message of peace from Rama." Saying thus, Angada entered Ravana's palace. Ravana was seated on a golden throne with ten shining diadems on his heads. Prahasta, his main counselor and commander-in-chief, was sitting at his feet with all the important friends, relatives, and military chiefs of his army seated in that great assembly. Just like Hanuman, Angada was fearless. As he was approaching boldly, singlehandedly, in the midst of the gathered throng, demon Ravana asked his commander-in-chief to handle the situation. Prahasta angrily stared at Angada and twisting his moustache, he commanded Angada to take his seat. Angada said he was comfortable standing and when asked the reason why he had come, Angada said, "I want to talk to Ravana directly about this situation."

Prahasta tried to insult Rama and Angada and then glorified Ravana. "O monkey," he said, "Ravana is the greatest being in all the three worlds. Thousands of celestial women are his slaves and all angels and archangels are his servants. Out of fear of him the sun shines, moon shines, and stars shine. Everything moves according to his will. He is the ruler of the three worlds. Agni the fire god cooks for him everyday. Indra brings timely rain for he is afraid of him and his son Indrajit. All the guardian deities and presiding deities over nature and planets just follow his commands. So salute my Lord Ravana, O Angada."

Hearing these words of Prahasta, Angada burst into laughter and spoke mockingly, "O Prahasta, a slave to glorify his lord is natural. You and your family and all these demons are fed by him and you glorify him for the sake of your position and possessions. I am a servant of God Rama; therefore, I need not salute or honor the thief who has stolen away Sita, but I would really like to see that Ravana who came disguisedly as a monk when Rama and Lakshmana were not in the hermitage and abducted Sita. Is this Ravana, whom you are praising, the same thief?

"I have heard about a Ravana who went to fight with my father Vali and was packed at the end of the tail and hung as a toy to my cradle. Even though many a time I hit him with my fist as a child, I don't exactly remember his face. Is he the same Ravana whom you are glorifying? I remember another story.

"There was a hero named Kartaveerya, who had one thousand arms. It is said he used to play in the water with his thousand queens. Once Ravana went there as they were playing in the water. When that hero, Kartaveerya, pulled the water by his thousand arms, Ravana was carried away by the currents in that river and was later imprisoned by Kartaveerya. When he was released, he came back to Lanka and declared that he had conquered Kartaveerya. Is that the same boastful demon who is your master?" Seeing Ravana's whole assembly getting angry at him, Angada looked directly at Ravana and addressed him, "Hey Ravana, aren't you the same Ravana who went to conquer the whole world, and struck by the beauty of a sagely women named Vedavati who was meditating to have God as her husband, you wanted to divert her meditation to marry you. When you went to touch her, she cursed you and flung herself in the fire by telling that if you touch any chaste woman, your head will be severed from the trunk."

Angada continued further, "Aren't you the same Ravana who went to the Himalayas, and arrogant as you were you wanted to lift Kailasa mountain of Lord Shiva, and while lifting you were caught in between the earth and the root of the mountain and began screaming and praying for protection? When Shiva blessed you and released you from that catastrophe, you returned from there and declared in Lanka that even Shiva was afraid of you while you lifted the Kailasa mountain. Aren't you the same Ravana who went to Rasatala, the nether region, where you wanted to conquer Bali, the immortal devotee of Vishnu and there Lord Vishnu himself was standing as the gatekeeper of his devotee? No sooner you saw him you were so terrified that without telling anybody, or fighting with Bali, didn't you just return to Lanka to tell everybody that you had conquered all the nether regions? O wretched demon, I can go on telling hundreds of stories so that all these people may know what an unrighteous and unworthy king you are. All these unrighteous deeds of yours culminated by abducting the Universal Mother, Sita, and all these sins will be forgiven by Rama through your one gesture of restoring Sita to him. Ravana, your younger brother Vibhishana has told you that Rama is God incarnate and Sita is goddess. Have no doubt about this. Without any more delay, offer Sita back to Rama."

Ravana was much infuriated by the merciless criticism of Angada. He asked everybody to listen to him, to be alert with swords and weapons, and to punish

Angada. Soldiers from all sides began using their weapons against Angada and in self-defense, Angada fought with them awhile, vanquished them, and finally he warned Ravana and all the demons that they would suffer the consequence for transgressing *dharma*. Rama sent Hanuman to bring Angada back safely. When Hanuman joined Angada, the demons were scattered out of fear of Hanuman. Both of them returned to Sri Rama and told him that Ravana would not listen to any word of compromise and war was inevitable.

The very next day, the war among monkeys and titans began. Demons fought ferociously and Rama's strength vanquished them. A heavy loss incurred on the side of the demons. Indrajit, son of Ravana, was very angry at this. He had many magic arrows with which he struck the monkey chieftains down. Finally, seeing all his magic becoming useless before the arrows of Rama and Lakshmana, he discharged a very powerful serpent arrow to bite and bind all *vaanaras*, Rama, and Lakshmana. Puffed with pride, Indrajit returned to Lanka and conveyed the message to Ravana. The entire night, when all *vaanaras* and Rama and Lakshmana were unconscious, only Vibhishana was going around in the battlefield, driving away fiends and goblins who had come to drink the blood of the monkeys. Early morning hours, Sri Rama returned to consciousness and cried like a child, seeing everybody, including Lakshmana, in that unconscious state. Suddenly he remembered his true nature as Mahavishnu and called Garuda, the eagle, which was his vehicle. When that huge bird, beating his wings, came there, those millions of serpents scattered in all directions. Garuda killed the serpents and released everybody. *Devas* showered flowers and this proved to everyone beyond doubt that Rama was none other than Mahavishnu. Garuda praised the Lord and returned to his abode. When all the monkeys disturbed the peace of the city by setting fire to Lanka, Indrajit and Ravana came to know that miraculously, all were saved and released from the serpent's arrow.

As the victory was gaining momentum, Ravana sent a demon named Dhumraksha with ten thousand demons to help him. He began driving all the *vaanaras* away. Seeing this, the diamond-bodied Hanuman faced him boldly, vanquished his troop, and finally in single combat, struck the demon with his fist. Dhumraksha vomited blood and departed to the abode of death. Then came Vajradamstra, a fierce demon, with his mighty troop. Angada faced him and a fierce battle ensued between the two. The powerful son of Vali gave the demons a taste of his fist and killed Vajradamstra.

Ravana sent Akampana who began causing terror among the monkeys. Seeing the powerful monkeys running away in the battlefield, Hanuman, the son of wind god, encouraged them to return to fight along with him. It took very little time for Hanuman to destroy Akampana. Neela, the son of fire god, was waiting for an opportunity to serve Rama. He saw Prahasta, the commander-in-chief of Ravana's army, coming to the battlefield with millions of demons. He attacked the camp of the monkeys and killed many of them. This outraged Neela, who fought with him gallantly and finally destroyed Prahasta. Ravana was very much grieved at the death of many important leaders of his army and wanted to show his prowess to Rama. Mounting on a golden chariot, Ravana, the terror of *devas*, drove away all the monkeys with his sharp arrows. Then came Rama, that Lord of gods, to fight with Ravana. Effortlessly, he vanquished the pride of Ravana and finally overcame him and destroying his chariot to pieces, held him captive. Merciful as he was, he advised Ravana to think again about his folly and return Sita to live happily. Ravana felt insulted and ran away from the battlefield.

Ravana's mother, Kaikasa, and his wife, Mandodari, time and again advised Ravana that until Sita was returned to Rama, there could be no peace. But Ravana would not listen to them or anybody. Arrogant as he was, he decided to awaken his sleeping brother, Kumbhakarna. It is said thousands of demons with different weapons in their hands, came to awaken Kumbhakarna. Once he sleeps, he wakes up only once in six months. To awaken him in the middle is a most difficult task and if at all he is awakened, then his death is certain. This was what Brahma had told him when he conferred his boon on him, as mentioned earlier. In this process of waking him, when the demons hit him by their weapons, it was like patting Kumbhakarna, who slept soundly. When some of the demons were turning hot iron rods in his ears, the demon felt so good, like the removing of ear wax, and never got up. Every form of effort to wake him up failed miserably. Finally, Brahma the creator, who gave him the boon, himself had to come. When he sprinkled water over him, then alone the demon awakened and roared. The entire city of Lanka trembled at that tumultuous noise. The demon was so hungry that thousands and thousands of animals and varieties of food were heaped in his presence. He finished the food in minutes and again roared that he was hungry. It was only Brahma the creator who made him drink the holy water and both his hunger and thirst were quenched. Decked with ornaments, that great hero among the demons came to the palace of Ravana. He was given extraordinary seat for him to sit comfortably. Even though ferocious to look at and mountainous in the size of his body, Kumbhakarna spoke the truth to Ravana.

"Ravana, you have awakened me at a wrong time. If you had waited until I completed my sleep, the army of Rama would have been eaten by me. Anyway, we cannot escape the inevitable. Tell me the reason for which I was awakened."

Ravana said, "O my dear brother, praising Rama, our youngest brother Vibhishana sought refuge in Rama. War was declared and one after another, the important leaders of our troop were killed by Rama's servants. Even though we also have destroyed many monkeys, still Rama's army is invincible. As you are the only hope of mine, I had to awaken you. I know you alone can devour Rama's army and kill Rama and Lakshmana."

Kumbhakarna said, "O my dear brother, I definitely feel that Rama is God, Sita is Goddess, and monkeys are the celestials. This seems to be a drama of God. You have done a wrong by abducting Sita, and the way to peace is to return her to Rama. I know this speech of mine will hurt your feelings, but I have spoken to you the truth as I see it. This does not mean that I am going to let you down. I shall fight the monkeys, Rama, and Lakshmana with all my strength, but I cannot assure you of success." Ravana gave him the permission to go to fight and return victorious.

Kumbhakarna's strength was beyond description. All the *vaanara* chiefs took to their heels and thousands of monkeys climbed all over his body, of which he was unaware. Drunk as he was, he captured Sugriva, the chief of monkeys, with one grip and hid him under his arm and returned to Ravana, but the clever Sugriva escaped from Kumbhakarna by tearing the tip of his nose with his nails, and returned to his camp. In that drunken state, Kumbhakarna was oblivious of this fact and he became aware of the escape of Sugriva only when he lifted his arm to show Sugriva to Ravana. Ravana rebuked him and the insulted Kumbhakarna returned with a troop of eighty thousand *rakshasas*, creating terror to the monkeys. Rama came out of his camp seeing the sad plight of his army and faced Kumbhakarna in battle. *Devas* glorified Rama, the one who had incarnated to destroy Ravana and Kumbhakarna. Now he began fulfilling the mission of his *avatar* by destroying the great hero Kumbhakarna.

As explained earlier, Ravana and Kumbhakarna were the two gatekeepers of Vishnu who had assumed the forms of the demons due to a curse uttered by the sages Sanaka and Sunandana. Now Kumbhakarna was slain by Rama. *Devas* praised Rama for the fulfillment of his promise. This was a great shock to Ravana. He thought his destruction was near. He disregarded the advice of his well-wishers once again and sent Narantaka to fight the *vaanaras*. When he heard Angada killed Narantaka, immediately he dispatched a huge army under the leadership of Devantaka, Mahodara, and Mahaparshva. In the beginning they vanquished Rama's army but finally they were all slain by the monkey chieftains.

There was another very great hero in Ravana's army known as Atikaya. He was a great devotee of Rama just like Vibhishana. He had never seen Rama physically, but when he was called to fight against Rama and Lakshmana by Ravana, Atikaya made all preparations to worship Rama through his battle. He welcomed all the *rakshasas* who wanted to go with him saying, "O beloved *rakshasas*, if you want to go across the ocean of rebirth, come with me to see Rama. Come everybody, those who want to attain freedom and eternal peace. This is the greatest opportunity; the eternal Lord is here with us. Let us attain the Kingdom of Heaven by fighting this battle as a worship to Rama." Leading a huge troop, Atikaya, the great devotee among the demons, came to fight and Sri Rama was so pleased with his devotion, that he decided not to fight with him. Finally, Lakshmana was sent by Rama and Atikaya offered his worship in the form of battle and reached the abode of God through the arrow of Lakshmana.

Ravana was grieved at this heavy loss but he never gave up the battle. He sent word to his great son, Indrajit, the invincible one. Indrajit encouraged his father that this time he would certainly kill Rama and Lakshmana along with all the *vaanaras*. Armed with celestial weapons and the missile of Brahma, adorned with celestial garlands, powerful Indrajit came to fight with a large number of titans. By the power of his magic, he took his chariot beyond the clouds and standing there, invisible, he discharged millions of arrows and made all the monkeys unconscious. Uttering the great *mantra* of Brahma, that son of Ravana discharged the missile of Brahma. The power of that missile was such that it bound everybody including Hanuman, Rama, and Lakshmana. Thus, vanquishing everybody, Indrajit returned to Lanka triumphantly.

At midnight there was only Vibhishana, again holding a burning torch in his hand, chanting the name of Rama, telling the evil spirits, "Scatter, scatter, in the name of Rama. Do not drink the blood of any monkey. You have no right to touch the bodies of the servants of Rama." Saying thus, that immortal votary of Rama was coming in search of someone who could guide him what to do. He found Brahma's son, Jambavan, the wise old man, lying on the battlefield. He told Vibhishana, "If you go further, you will meet Hanuman. Even though Hanuman is also caught by the missile of Brahma, due to the boon which he has, he will be released from the missile. But Hanuman needs someone to remind him of his strength. So glorify him and bring him to me. I will tell him the secret."

As per the instruction of Jambavan, Vibhishana went to Hanuman. Like a huge mountain, bound by a thick rope, Hanuman was bound by Brahma's missile and he was chanting, "Rama, Rama." When Vibhishana reminded him of his strength, Hanuman emerged out of bondage and along with Vibhishana, he came to Jambavan. Jambavan instructed him to go to the Himalayas where he would find a rare type of medicinal herb which restores life to the dead, known as *Amrita-sanjeevani*.

"Hanuman," Jambavan said, "if you could bring that herb by morning, we will be able to restore all back to life. Once the morning sun rises, then we will become helpless. Hurry, O son of wind. Nothing is impossible for you." Glorified thus by Jambavan, Hanuman took a leap to that mountain in the Himalayas. He made a thorough search for that medicinal herb. As it was getting late, Hanuman thought of plucking the whole mountain. Accordingly, the size of his body grew and wrapping his tail around that mountain, that illustrious monkey brought the whole mountain containing the herbs to the battlefield.

First of all, the wise Jambavan searched for the herb, the juice of which was sprinkled in the eyes of Sushena, the physician of the monkeys. When he got up, he took the necessary *Sanjeevani* herbs and applied their juice to the eyes of all including Rama and Lakshmana, who got up during the early morning hours, as if they were awakened from sleep. The dutiful Hanuman, as per the instruction of Jambavan, took that mountain back to the Himalayas and placed it where it had been. That glorious devotee of Rama, thereafter returned to Rama and made all very happy.

Once again the trumpets and kettledrums were played and Rama's army set fire to Lanka. Ravana and Indrajit were sleeping happily, thinking that all were slain in Rama's army. To their utter amazement, when they came to know that all of them had returned to life, Ravana was very depressed. He sent two fierce demons named Kumbha and Nikumbha. Playfully, Angada killed Kumbha and Hanuman destroyed Nikumbha. Having all his efforts fail, Ravana again sent Indrajit to weaken the strength of Rama. Indrajit, through his magic, created a mimic figure of Sita and showing it to Rama on the battlefield, he said, "Rama, here is your chaste wife, Sita. We tolerated her unwillingness by appealing to her in hundreds of ways to forget you and marry Ravana. She maintained her patience until now. Now she has taken a decision which she is going to tell you." Saying thus, he placed that figure which had the likeness of Sita before Rama. That figure cried and spoke to Rama, thus, "Rama, I am your unfortunate wife, Sita. It is useless to fight Indrajit and Ravana. Their power is immense and I advise you to go back to Ayodhya without me. Indrajit is going to kill me unless I agree to marry his father, Ravana. I have come to tell you, you may withdraw the battle and return to Ayodhya. You may completely forget about me." As she was crying, Indrajit challenged Rama and cut off the head of Sita's figure. This caused a great agony to Rama for some time. Immediately, Vibhishana told Rama that all this was done by the magic of Indrajit. As the fierce arrows of Rama began springing from his quiver, Indrajit was unnerved and ran away from the battlefield, as his magical powers disappeared like the mist before the sun. He went to the nether regions and began a very powerful fire-sacrifice known as *Nikumbhila Yaga*. As he was performing that fire-sacrifice, offering oblations in the fire, the miraculous powers came to him, and if only one day would have been left to continue that fire-sacrifice, he would have obtained the grace of war goddess and then no one could vanquish him in the battle. Fortunately, Vibhishana reminded Rama that within twenty-four hours, Indrajit should be killed. Once he completes the *yaga*, then it is impossible to slay him. "But my Lord," Vibhishana continued, "it requires a person who is a celibate, and who has never slept for fourteen years, nor sipped even a drop of water for fourteen years. No one other than such an austere person, could kill him." Sri Rama became perplexed and looked around for such a man. To his wonder, his brother, Lakshmana, came forward and fell at the feet of Rama. "My Lord," he said, "I, your servant, am ready to fight with Indrajit." Rama said, "My son, didn't you sleep all these fourteen years? Didn't you eat or drink all these years? Then how did you live?" Lakshmana said, "Prabho, your *seva* gave me all strength. Your grace made me practice this austerity all these years." Sri Rama and all the *vaanaras* were in tears seeing that strong devotion of the immortal Lakshmana.

Lakshmana was like a flagstaff. People glorify the flag but who composes any song on the staff? It is the sacrifice of the staff which makes the flag fly in the sky. Lakshmana stood strong like that flagstaff to make the flag of Rama's glory fly forever. Such was his sacrifice.

Armed with the necessary weapons and the blessings of Rama, accompanied by Hanuman and Vibhishana, that illustrious brother of Ramachandra went to the nether regions where Indrajit was performing *Nikumbhila Yaga*. When only a few hours were left for the completion of the *yaga*, Hanuman and Lakshmana disturbed his meditation. If he became angry, then all the fruits of his labor would be gone. Unfortunately, the disturbance caused by Hanuman made him lose his temper. Then a fierce battle took place. It shook the three worlds. The power of the austerity of Lakshmana destroyed all his magical powers until finally, he destroyed the chariot, bow, and arrows of Indrajit. That immortal brother of Rama finally twanged his bow and fixed a powerful dart, which he discharged over Indrajit. That shaft took his life away by cutting off Indrajit's head. As this removed the fear of the *devas*, they showered flowers. Hanuman brought the head of Indrajit and threw it in the palace of Ravana. Sri Rama warmly embraced Lakshmana and praised his sacrifice for the protection of *dharma*.

Ravana's grief completely weakened him. Mandodari wept bitterly and told him, "My lord, you have lost everything because of your ego and your wrong desires. Still it is not too late. Wise as you are, why don't you decide to return Rama's wife to him?" Ravana said, "Mandodari, it is too late to take such a decision. I have lost all my children, relatives, and friends. Do you want me to be a coward and escape from the battlefield? I know my prowess. I shall retaliate and take away the life of Lakshmana as he has taken the life of my son, Indrajit.

Then I will slay Rama. I shall never go back from this decision." Saying thus, that stubborn demon, with one hundred thousand well-trained, demoniac soldiers, marched to the battlefield, carrying the celestial weapons.

Ravana drove away the greatest of the monkey chieftains until finally, Lakshmana faced him. Even though Lakshmana humbled the pride of Ravana, the titan cleverly hit a very powerful shaft to the bosom of Lakshmana which made him then and there fall on the ground unconscious. Taking that as an opportunity, the mighty Ravana jumped down from his chariot and with an evil intention of carrying Lakshmana's body away, tried to lift his body. As Lakshmana was the *avatar* of Mahashesha, the energy that holds the entire universe, the demon failed in his efforts to lift his body. As he was struggling to carry the body away, the sagacious monkey, Hanuman, saw this and with his diamond fist he hit on the head of Ravana in such a way that the demon whirled around thrice and drove away, out of fear of Hanuman, on his chariot back to Lanka. Hanuman shed tears of grief at the loss of that illustrious Lakshmana and carried his seemingly dead body back to the camp of Sri Rama. Sri Rama sank in the ocean of grief remembering the divine attributes of Lakshmana.

Out of great agony, Rama cried, "O brother Lakshmana, awake, arise. Kindly open your eyes. Look at me once. Are you angry with me that I am so attached to Sita? Lakshmana, you are dearer to me than Sita. You are more than my life. Without you, I cannot go back to Ayodhya. You suffered for me endlessly. For fourteen years, without sipping a drop of water or taking any rest, you lived a life of great austerity. O my beloved brother, why are you silent today? That cruel fate brought us to the forest and brought us various troubles, but I was able to withstand all these difficulties because of your loving service. Lakshmana, will you forgive me and once again return to life? What shall I tell your mother and your wife? Oh, why should I fight anymore? Let that cruel fate take away my life as well. I cannot live without you."

Seeing Rama's grief, Hanuman and all the monkey chieftains cried bitterly. Both Jambavan and Sushena once again requested Hanuman to rush to the Himalayas to bring the same medicinal herb by morning. Even though only a few hours were left, the son of wind flew to the Himalayas and began searching for the same herb on that mountain. To his wonder, when he went near that herb, it went far away from him and again he tried and found that it was beyond his reach. Finally, that formidable monkey used his tail to lift the mountain as he did before. As he was bringing the mountain, he was so fatigued and thirsty, he wanted to drink some water. Nearby he found a beautiful *ashram* with a wonderful lake. It was not there the previous time he had been there. There was no time for Hanuman to think. As he was very thirsty, he came to the lake and along with the mountain hanging to his tail, that illustrious monkey jumped into the lake and felt very cool and relaxed. He drank water to his heart's content and by the time he finished drinking, his head began reeling, eyes began swimming, and he felt he was going to die.

Unfortunately, to add to his misfortune, a crocodile caught him by the foot and went on swallowing him, along with the mountain. But for the chant of "Rama," which his tongue was continuously repeating at that time, there was no other power to protect him; and without Rama's blessing, which had made him deathless, he would have died. Only a little consciousness was left with him. Hanuman prayed to Sri Ramachandra while he was entering into the mouth of the crocodile. This gave him enough strength to remember his mission. Chanting the name of Rama, Hanuman grew the size of his body until the body of the crocodile burst and he came out. As he was coming up from the lake, he saw a celestial woman emerging out of the body of the crocodile. She blessed Hanuman and said, "Hey Maruti, I am a celestial nymph named Dhyanamalani. Once when I came to bathe in a lake, demon Ravana chastised me and spoiled me. Thus was born a son named Atikaya. My husband angrily uttered a curse due to which I became a crocodile. He rescinded the curse by saying, 'When you meet the servant of Rama, you will be restored to your original purity.' Today, Hanuman, by holding your feet I was relieved from the crocodile body. This lake and the atmosphere here was pure and clean before. Knowing that you would come here to take the medicinal herbs as you did before, the clever Ravana has sent a demon here named Kalanemi, who is sitting disguised as a sage under that tree. He has poisoned the waters of the lake and the atmosphere here to cause your death. Now you can destroy that demon and restore the peace of this place." Saying thus, Dhyanamalini ascended to the celestial abode. Hanuman came to that demon who was posing as if meditating and lifting him up by his feet and whirling him round and round, he dashed him to the ground and killed him. Immediately the poisonous atmosphere was purified. Thereafter, Hanuman, carrying the mountain, flew in a hurry.

Back in Ayodhya, Rama's brother Bharata was sleepless that night and as he was gazing at the sky, he saw the huge body of Hanuman carrying a mountain. He mistook him to be a demon and hit him with a powerful shaft. Along with the mountain, Hanuman fell on the ground, chanting, "Rama, Rama." Hearing the Holy Name of Rama, Bharata thought that he had committed a sin. He came running to Hanuman, removing the shaft from his body. He asked Hanuman who he was. Hanuman opened his eyes and saw Bharata. He mistook Bharata to be Rama, as Bharata was clad in bark garments and matted locks. Hanuman was confused and asked Bharata who he was. When he said that he was Bharata, the younger brother of Rama, Hanuman disclosed his identity and narrated the past events in short and asked Bharata's permission to return to Rama, without which the life of Lakshmana shall not be restored.

Receiving the blessings of Bharata, Hanuman flew to Lanka, carrying the mountain of *Sanjeevani* herbs. He reached there in time and physician Sushena plucked the herbs and squeezed its juice into the eyes of Lakshmana. During the early morning hours, Lakshmana regained consciousness and was completely recovered. This brought strength and peace to Sri Rama.

Again the battle began. Ravana's army was routed in the battle. Ravana had to call his last remaining division of army. His wife, Mandodari, and mother, Kaikasa, appealed to him as a last effort, which failed. The strong, determined demon Ravana gave a gallant battle with Rama. He covered all the waters with his shafts. Through his magical powers, he created pitch darkness everywhere. It was at that time the immortal sage, Agastya, came to Rama and taught him a great prayer on light called "Aditya-hridaya." "Rama," the sage said, "with this prayer you can dispel the darkness created by Ravana and all his magical powers. Please hold the bow of Vishnu which I gave you in my *ashram*. Discharging your arrow through that bow, you shall slay Ravana." So saying, the sage departed to his abode. Rama chanted the prayer and the bright sun manifested, completely dispelling the darkness. Ravana's magical powers were also destroyed.

As a last effort, Ravana disappeared from the battle-field and went to the nether regions to perform a *yaga* called *Patala-homa*. At the advice of Vibhishana, Hanuman went there, pulling Ravana's wife Mandodari by the tuft of her hair. This disturbed Ravana and his meditation very much, so leaving the fire-sacrifice, along with Mandodari, Ravana came back to his palace. Rama's shafts began cutting the heads of Ravana. Immediately in their place, the new heads would emerge. This confused Rama and at that time Vibhishana revealed the secret, saying, "Sri Rama, Ravana has in his heart a celestial vessel of nectar called *Amrita-kalasha*. Until that is taken out, so long Ravana cannot die." Now Sri Rama hit at the bosom of Ravana and took away the vessel containing the nectar. Now Ravana remembered the words of Vibhishana, that Rama is God. He remembered his past life as the gatekeeper of Lord Vishnu. Giving up all his demoniac qualities, Ravana joined his twenty palms together and gazing at Rama's celestial personality, entered into great ecstasy. Now the sharp arrows of Rama cut off the heads one by one until he was left with one head and two arms. Ravana glorified Sri Rama and said, "Rama, but for my bringing Sita here, you would not have come. Even though I brought Sita, I have never touched her and have kept her away from my palace in the Ashoka grove. To end my curse, you have taken *avatar*. I am happy I fought with you and now I am ready to return to your abode." Saying thus, Ravana accepted the will of God as Rama's arrow severed his head from his trunk. Trumpets sounded, sages chanted *Vedic mantras*, Narada and Tumbara sang the *kirtans*. Celestials showered flowers. Celestial nymphs danced and all fourteen worlds were happy because they were relieved of the agony caused by the demon.

Mandodari and the queens of Ravana cried bitterly and Rama consoled them. Mandodari, being a very chaste wife, was glorified by Rama, who blessed her, saying, "O Mandodari, you have been very devoted to your husband, therefore, your name will be remembered throughout eternity."

Rama consoled Vibhishana and asked him to perform the funeral rites of Ravana, Kumbhakarna, and others. Vibhishana performed the obsequies. Seeing an auspicious moment, Sri Rama installed Vibhishana on the throne of Lanka. Thereafter, Vibhishana brought Sita to Sri Rama. To the wonder of everybody, Rama ordered

Hanuman to collect fuel and light it. When the fire was ablaze, Rama asked Sita to fling herself into the fire to testify to the world of her purity. All the *vaanaras* cried at this, but Sita, who was conscious of her purity, came round the fire thrice and said, "O Agni, the fire god, if I am pure in thought, word, and deed; in mind, speech, and body; if I have never thought of any man in the place of Rama even in my dreams, then alone send me back alive. Otherwise, let my body be reduced to ashes." Saying thus, that embodiment of chastity, that immortal wife of Rama, flung herself into the fire. Not even a petal of the flower that which was fixed to her hair faded. The fire god told Rama and everyone Sita was pure. The fire of her chastity burnt even the fire god. All the *devas* glorified the Universal Mother. From the ancestral kingdom, Rama's father, Dasharatha, appeared on the scene and blessed Sita and Rama. He glorified Sita and asked Rama to accept her. To the joy of everybody, Sri Ramachandra accepted Sita. Celestial music sounded everywhere and Indra, the head of the angels, told Rama to ask for any favor. Rama said, "Let all those *vaanaras* who died during the battle be restored to life." Accordingly, Indra restored the lives of the dead monkeys.

Vibhishana offered his Pushpaka Vimana. All the monkeys, Rama, Lakshmana, Sita, and Vibhishana, sat in that aerial car to return to Ayodhya. On their way, Rama described different places to Sita and met Bharadvaja awhile. As it was already the last day of the fourteen years, Sri Rama sent Hanuman to Bharata. Otherwise, Bharata would kill himself by plunging into the fire. Hanuman rushed to Ayodhya and saw Bharata making preparation to throw himself into the fire, for that was the stipulation he made with Rama long ago. When Hanuman conveyed the news of Rama's arrival, Bharata became very happy and gave up the thought of throwing himself into the fire. The news spread to all of Ayodhya.

A new life came to everybody. Kausalya's joy knew no bounds. The entire Ayodhya rose to receive Sri Rama and lo, the Pushpaka Vimana descended and Rama emerged with Lakshmana and Sita. There was a deafening noise of "Jai to Sri Rama, Sita, and Lakshmana!" Bharata and Shatrughna embraced Sri Rama. Mother Kausalya blessed Rama. Kaikeyi and Sumitra again and again blessed Rama, Lakshmana, and Sita.

Immediately, all the preparations were made for the coronation of Rama. Brahma-rishi Vasishta and Minister Sumantra, organized everything. At the most auspicious hour, the coronation ceremony took place. Sita on the left, Lakshmana on the right, Bharata and Shatrughna on either side, and Hanuman at Rama's feet. Sri Rama gave the *Divine Darshan* to all the devotees. Rama ruled over the kingdom of Ayodhya righteously and brought the Kingdom of Heaven on earth.

Whosoever reads or recites, narrates or listens to this immortal epic of Rama, shall realize the Truth and attain prosperity and peace, joy and immortality, here and hereafter. Sage Valmiki sang this song and taught it to Rama's children, Lava and Kusha, who made the Ramayana popular. Tulasidas, Narahari, Kamban and others, have retold the story of Rama in millions of ways and the essence of all these is written here as a humble effort to illumine our Western readers. May the devotees use this book as a scripture for daily reading, in family circles, for children, and for adults, so that the blessings of Sita and Rama may make every family peaceful and noble. May the entire world be filled with peace and so be it.

BOOK VII

UTTARA KANDA

Sri Rama ruled over Ayodhya for many, many years. During his reign, there was timely rain, abundant grains, fruits, milk, and honey. All were devotees of Rama and followed his example. Therefore, people were very righteous, healthy, long-lived, and were happy. During Rama's rule, law and justice prevailed, not only for human beings but also for animals. Rama himself heard the complaints and dealt justly. The following story proves this.

Once it so happened a dog was sleeping by the side of the road. A priest, who was passing by, hit the dog's head with a stick for no reason. The bleeding dog came near the hall of justice, pulled the string and rang a huge bell to lodge a complaint before Rama. Rama came to the hall with Sita and his brothers and there he saw the bleeding dog. The dog said, "My Lord, in your kingdom, it is said that law and justice prevail, but today, as I was resting by the roadside, a priest hit me on my head without any wrongdoing on my part. I want you to duly punish him for his wrong."

Hearing these words of the animal, Rama sent his messengers to bring that priest to the hall of justice. When the priest was brought, he admitted before Rama that he had hit the dog. Rama questioned the dog, "What punishment to the priest would please you?" The dog said, "Rama, make him the high priest of a huge monastery. That is the proper punishment for this man."

Hearing these words of the dog, all were astonished. Rama called the dog to explain. The dog said, "My Lord, in my past life, I was high priest of a large monastery. That power corrupted me and I deceived the public by misusing my powers. Due to transgression of my *dharma*, I was punished to be born as a dog in this life. So, if you make this man a high priest, he will do what I did and then he will be reborn as a dog like me and will be hit on the head by someone else. Is that not a proper punishment?"

Hearing the words of the dog, everyone laughed. The priest begged Rama to forgive him. Rama healed the dog and forgave the priest. Ultimately, Rama gave both of them the immortal Kingdom of Heaven.

In *Uttara Kanda*, the birth, growth, and the powers of the *rakshasas* and demon Ravana, is explained. Also, Sri Rama sends pregnant Sita with Lakshmana to Sage Valmiki's *ashram*. There she gives birth to the twins, Lava and Kusha. Sage Valmiki teaches Sita's two children the immortal Ramayana.

Once Rama wanted to perform Ashwamadha-Yoga, or a horse-sacrifice. As per the scriptural ordinance, Rama had to send that special horse, along with his troop, around the country. The stipulation was, a king of each state should offer their tribute no sooner they see the horse, or they should bind the horse to wage a war with Rama's troop. Almost every state in India, no sooner they saw the horses of Rama and his troop, offered their tribute. In its wanderings, when the horse came to Valmiki's *ashram*, the bold twins, Lava and Kusha, bound the horse, without knowing it was the horse of their father. They fought a severe battle and located the troop of Rama. They also made Lakshmana, Bharata, and Shatrughna unconscious. Finally, Rama himself had to fight and they gave him a difficult time until Sage

Valmiki intervened and told Lava and Kusha that Rama was their father, whose story they sang everyday. The sage also told Rama the twins were his children, born in the *ashram*.

As it was time for Sita and Rama to depart to their transcendental abode, Rama sent for Sita. As Sita saluted Rama, Mother Earth opened and received Sita, as she was the daughter of the earth, having been found by Janaka in the furrow.

Thereupon, Rama returned to Ayodhya, performed the horse-sacrifice, and blessed humanity.

Sage Agastya and all the Himalayan masters came to Sri Rama and requested him to return to His transcendental abode of Vaikunta. As his mission on earth was finished, that immortal Lord decided to return to Vaikunta.

On the bank of Sarayu River, all seventy-two million monkeys assumed their angelic forms and Rama assumed the form of Lord Vishnu, holding Bharata as his conch, and Shatrughna as his discus. Lakshmana assumed his serpent-god form. Then his vehicle, Garuda, the eagle, descended from Vaikunta to take Rama. Simultaneously, millions of aerial cars descended from celestial regions.

Mounting on Garuda, Rama blessed the earth and humanity, saying, "I have placed My power in My Holy Name and in the book, Ramayana. Whosoever chants My Holy Name and reads My story, will receive My blessings, and all his wishes shall be fulfilled on earth. Ultimately, he should attain My transcendental abode. My story will inspire humanity and will last as long as mountains stand and rivers flow. Wherever Ramayana is sung or read, I shall dwell there. Whosoever chants My name, I make his heart My abode." Saying thus, Sri Ramachandra, who had assumed the form of Vishnu, ascended to Vaikunta. Thereafter, all the angels returned to their abodes.

As it is the tradition in India to stop reading and reciting Ramayana at the coronation of Rama, we have not elaborated on the story contained in this seventh book. The reason for this tradition is to feel God's presence on earth forever. Still I have mentioned the seventh book very briefly, to tell our readers how the story ends.

This is a very humble attempt in narrating the story of Rama. As Sant Tulasidas says, "Even though the seven oceans were made into ink, and the Himalaya mountains became the pen, still one cannot finish the endless glory of Sri Rama." Therefore, the story which I have narrated is just a drop from the nectarian ocean of the glory of Rama.

Even though you drink a drop of nectar, you will attain the same immortality had you drunk the entire ocean.

Full of reverence and devotion, read Ramayana a few pages every day, write Rama Mantra at least one page every day, and do *japa* of Taraka Mantra.

May Sri Rama and Sita bless you with devotion and liberation. May Lord Hanuman bless you with courage, strength, longevity, and *bhakti*. May the entire universe be filled with love and peace.

Raghuramachandra Maharajaki Jai

SITA RAMA RAMA SITA RAM

Sita Rama Rama Sita Ram
Sita Rama Rama Sita Ram

(1) God incarnated as Rama
Showed the way, truth, and the life
Goddess incarnated as Sita
To show the happy married life
(Refrain)

(2) Rama was the perfect man
Sita was perfect woman
Rama taught us Divine Love
Sita taught how to forgive
(Refrain)

(3) Lakshmana taught to work with peace
Bharata taught selfless service
Shatrughna taught power of silence
Hanuman taught how to become a Das
(Refrain)

(4) Chant this mantra with all Prem
Sri Ram Jai Ram Jai Jai Ram
You will attain the highest wisdom
Health and wealth, peace and freedom
(Refrain)

RAMAYANA IN SONG

Shuddha Brahma Parātpara Rama
Kālātmaka Paramēshvara Rama
Sheshatalpa Sukha nidrita Rama
Brahmādyamara Prārthita Rama
Chanda Kirana Kula Mandana Rama
Srimad Dasharatha Nandana Rama
Kausalya Sukhavardhana Rama
Vishvāmitra Priyadhana Rama
Ghora Tatakā Ghātaka Rama
Māreechādi Nipātaka Rama
Kaushika Makha Samrakshaka Rama
Srimad Ahalyoddhāraka Rama
Gautama Muni Sampujita Rama
Suramuni Varagana Samstuta Rama
Nāvika Dhāvita Mridupada Rama
Mithilā Purajana Mohaka Rama
Videha Mānasa Ranjaka Rama
Tryambaka Kārmuka Bhanjaka Rama
Sitārpita Vara Mālika Rama
Krita Vaivāhika Kautuka Rama
Bhārgava Darpa Viñashaka Rama
Srimad Ayodhyā Pālaka Rama
Aganita Gunagana Bhushita Rama
Avani Tanayā Kāmita Rama
Rākā Chandra Samānana Rama
Pitri Vākyāshrita Kānana Rama
Priya Guha Vinivedita Pada Rama
Tatkshālita Nija Mridupada Rama

Bharadvāja Mukhānandaka Rama
Chikrakootādri Niketana Rama
Dasharatha Santata Chintita Rama
Kaikeyi Tanayārthita Rama
Virachita Nija Pitri Karmaka Rama
Bharatārpita Nija Pāduka Rama
Dandakavanajana Pāvana Rama
Dusta Virādha Vināshana Rama
Sharabhanga Suteekshnārchita Rama
Agastyānugraha Vardhita Rama
Gridhrādhipa Samsevita Rama
Panchavati Tata Susthita Rama
Shoorpanakhārti Vidhāyaka Rama
Khara Dushana Mukha Sudaka Rama
Sitāpriya Harinānuga Rama
Mareechārti Kridāshuga Rama
Vinasta Sitānveshaka Rama
Gridhrādhipa Gatidāyaka Rama
Shabaridatta Phalāshana Rama
Kabandha Bahucchedana Rama
Hanumatsevita Nijapada Rama
Nata Sugrivābheestada Rama
Garvita Vāli Samhāraka Rama
Vānara Duta Preshaka Rama
Hitakara Lakshmana Samyuta Rama
Kapivara Santata Samsmrita Rama
Tadgati Vighna Dhvamsaka Rama
Sita Prānādhāraka Rama
Dusta Dashānana Dushita Rama
Shista Hanumad Bhushita Rama
Sita Vedita Kāvana Rama
Krita Chudāmani Darshana Rama
Kapivara Vachanāshvāsita Rama
Rāvana Nidhana Prastita Rama
Vanara Sainya Samāvrita Rama
Shoshita Sharadheeshārthita Rama

Vibhishanābhaya Dāyaka Rama
Parvata Setunibandhaka Rama
Kumbhakarna Shiraschedaka Rama
Rākshaka Sangha Vimardaka Rama
Ahimahi Rāvana Chārana Rama
Samhrita Dashamukha Rāvana Rama
Vidhibhavamukha Sura Samstuta Rama
Khastita Dasharatha Veekshita Rama
Sitādarshana Modita Rama
Abhishikta Vibhishana Nata Rama
Pushpakayānārohana Rama
Bharadvājābhinishevana Rama
Bharata Prāna Priyakara Rama
Sāketapuri Bhushana Rama
Sakala Sveeya Samānata Rama
Ratnala Satpeetāsthita Rama
Pattābhishekalānkrita Rama
Pārthiva Kula Sammānita Rama
Vibhishanārpita Rangaka Rama
Keeshakulānugrihakara Rama
Sakala Jiva Samrakshaka Rama
Samasta Lokādhāraka Rama
Rama Rama Jaya Raja Ram
Rama Rama Jaya Sita Ram
Agata Munigana Samstuta Rama
Vishruta Dashakantodbhava Rama
Sitālingana Nirvrita Rama
Neeti Surakshita Janapada Rama
Vipina Tyājita Janakaja Rama
Kārita Lavanāsura Vadha Rama
Svargata Shambhooka Samstuta Rama
Svatanaya Kushalāvanandita Rama
Ashvamedha Kritu Deekshita Rama
Kālāvedita Surapada Rama
Ayodhyakajana Muktida Rama
Vidhimukha Vibudhānandaka Rama

Tejomaya Nija Roopaka Rama
Samsriti Bandha Vimochaka Rama
Dharmasthāpana Tatpara Rama
Bhakti Parāyana Muktida Rama
Sarvacharāchara Pālaka Rama
Sarva Bhavāmaya Vāraka Rama
Vaikuntālaya Samsthita Rama
Nityānanda Padasthita Rama
Rama Rama Jaya Raja Rama
Rama Rama Jaya Sita Rama
Bhayahara Mangala Dasharatha Rama
Jaya Jaya Mangala Sita Rama
Mangalakara Jaya Mangala Rama
Sangata Shubhavibhavodaya Rama
Anandamrita Varshaka Rama
Āshritavatsala Jaya Jaya Rama
Raghupati Rāghava Rāja Rama
Patita Pāvana Sita Rama
Om Shanti Shanti Shanti

"Ramayana is the guide for practical, happy life here and hereafter. Sri Rama is God incarnate, perfect man; and Sita is Goddess incarnate, perfect woman. Ramayana teaches divine love in practical life and is a guidebook for all married people, as it deals with happy marriage. Ramayana means 'the way in which Rama walked' or 'the path of perfection shown by Sri Rama.' A daily reading of this book brings the blessings of wisdom, love, and peace. May Sri Rama and Sita bless all."

–Sadguru Sant Keshavadas

Sadguru Sant Keshavadas is a prophet of divine love and universal peace. His name means "saint who is the servant of the Lord."

Sri Sadguru was born in 1934 in Bhadragiri, a small South Indian village near Bangalore in Karnataka State. He earned a B.A. degree from Mahatma Gandhi College, an L.L.B. degree from Udipi Law College, and is a gifted composer, musician, lecturer, author, and teacher of yoga.

Through the ancient wisdom of the Himalayas, he tries to unite all the world religions into Vishwa Dharma, or Cosmic Religion. In his mission to show the essential unity of all world religions, Sant Keshavadas has made nine global tours. His devoted wife Srimathi Rama Mata and their three children assist in this mission.

In 1961 Sant Keshavadas established Dasashram International Center in Bangalore, India, and since then has established other ashrams, meditation centers, and temples of Cosmic Religion all over the world.